THE RELEVANT LIFE OF MOSES

WHY ARE WE STILL ASKING PHARAOH?
LET OUR PEOPLE GO!

Wayne E. Croft Sr., DMin, PhD

© 2022 Heritage Publishing

All rights reserved. No portion of this book may be reproduced, stored in a retrieval system, or transmitted in any form or by any means—electronic, mechanical, photocopying, recorded, scanning, or other—except for brief quotations in critical reviews or articles, without the prior written permission of the publisher.

New Revised Standard Version, Updated Edition, Copyright 2021 National Council of Churches of Christ in the United States of America. Used by permission. All rights reserved worldwide.

All photographs and captions in this resource are from Wikimedia Commons, the free media repository, and are in public domain.

978-0-998-77667-5

Printed in the United States of America.

THE RELEVANT LIFE OF MOSES

WHY ARE WE STILL ASKING PHARAOH?
LET OUR PEOPLE GO!

Contents

Introduction 7

Lesson 1: Providence, Problems, and Promise 9

Lesson 2: Broken But Not Useless 28

Lesson 3: Go Down, Moses 47

Lesson 4: Let My People Go 66

Lesson 5: The Plagues 85

Lesson 6: Saved by the Blood 101

Lesson 7: Not So Fast 118

Lesson 8: The God Who Fights Our Battles 134

Lesson 9: The Bitter Into Sweet 151

Lesson 10: Everyone Needs a Jethro 167

Lesson 11: Experiencing God's Glory 180

Lesson 12: The Tragedy of a Missed Opportunity 197

Lesson 13: Finishing Well 221

Introduction

As students of Scripture, we've read about Moses leading the children of Israel through the wilderness. We've rejoiced when they crossed the Red Sea on dry ground, escaping Pharaoh's army. We've condemned them for their disobedience in the wilderness. We know how the story ends, so we might not stick around for their entrance into the Promised Land.

But Moses' life was complex and filled with contradictions, and it's impossible to understand this great prophet and leader without the context of his history or without becoming acquainted with the people he led. Not only is their story a fascinating account of God's power and faithfulness, but historically there have been many connections made between the enslaved Israelites and those persons who were enslaved here in the United States. We have had our share of wilderness experiences as we have searched for own version of the Promised Land.

As we study the life of Moses, we will walk through the Book of Exodus. We'll witness Pharaoh's wrath and the infant Moses' escape from near death. We'll see Moses' flight from Egypt and then meet him years later at the burning bush. After God's call to Moses to lead God's people out of slavery in Egypt, we'll walk alongside the Israelites as they cross the Red

Sea, praising God for destroying their enemies, only to complain later to Moses about the water, the food, and his leadership. Along the way, we'll explore some of the connections between the enslaved Israelites and the enslaved in America through pre-Civil War history and Negro Spirituals. We'll also study archaeological and historical information that will give us a greater sense of place and time in the ancient Near East.

When we look over the expanse of our lives, we may find similarities with Moses. We can probably think of our greatest victories and triumphs, while also remembering our lowest moments and sorrows. Our lives, like Moses', is bittersweet. He was a prince of the pharaonic palace only to become a fugitive. God called him out of the fields of Midian to lead millions of people out of slavery, but he wasn't allowed to enter the Promised Land. His life serves as both an inspiration and a cautionary tale, but he leaves a lasting legacy and an indelible impression on our Christian faith.

As you embark on this study, I pray that, like Moses, you will hear God's voice and answer God's call to do great things for the Kingdom. Whether you are studying with a small-group Bible study, a Sunday school class, or alone in your personal time with God, may your study of Moses' life enrich your spiritual life and draw you closer to the Lord.

1

Lesson 1
Providence, Problems, and Promise
Focus Scripture: Exodus 1:8–2:10

An Auspicious Life Begins

Many of us have read the Scriptures about Moses, so we're quite familiar with his story. We probably know that Pharaoh wanted to destroy all baby boys born in Egypt at that time and that Moses' mother went to great lengths to prevent her son from being one of Pharaoh's victims. We know how Moses ended up in Pharaoh's palace, but also how he ended up fleeing Egypt as a wanted man. But we know that despite setbacks, he went on to be a great leader. We also know the end of his story, which is at once sad and inspirational.

For African Americans, Moses' story is particularly poignant. For many of our enslaved ancestors, Moses and the children of Israel were a source of hope. If God could deliver the Israelites out of slavery in Egypt after 400 years, certainly God could do it for an enslaved people in America.

As we begin our study of the life of Moses, we'll go all the way back to the beginning. But keep in mind that's not where God started the story, and that's not where God starts our story. Although we are constrained by the limits of time—specifically when we're born and when we die—God exists in eternity, so God's not restricted by the parameters of human life and death. God made plans for Moses, and for us, long before birth.

Moses' life was lived out in three distinct phases of 40 years each. In this lesson, we will begin our study at the beginning in an Egypt ruled by a king who no longer protected God's people or respected their God. Moses was born in chaos and unrest, but divine providence would position him to be a great leader and accomplish God's will for God's people.

1. What do you already know about Moses and his story?

2. What inspiration can you glean from your current knowledge of Moses' life?

3. Have you heard older generations refer to Moses and the children of Israel as a source of hope in times of oppression and injustice? How might that inspire you today?

Providence

In his book *The Invisible Hand of God*, R. C. Sproul elaborates on what scholars refer to as "the providence of God." *Providence* is a big religious word, not easily understood, and it appears to be slowly vanishing from the vocabulary of contemporary Christians. Many Christians prefer to talk about God's provisions rather than God's providence. However, God's provisions come first through God's providence.

To speak of God's providence is to say that God sees the end and purpose for what happens in our lives. It is not merely that God *looks* at human affairs, but rather that God *looks after* human affairs. God *watches* us but also *watches over* us. In God's providence, God rules creation with absolute sovereignty and authority. God governs everything that comes to pass, from the greatest to the least, and nothing ever happens beyond the scope of God's divine will and purpose.

God raises up kingdoms and brings them down. God numbers the hairs on our heads and the days of our lives. God is in complete control of the universe and all who inhabit it. But trusting in God's providence can be one of the hardest lessons for us to learn, particularly when we find ourselves in the midst of uncertainty and chaos or when life takes us in directions we do not wish to go. And herein lies the story of the birth and life of Moses, as well as the story of the Israelites' journey from enslavement in Egypt to freedom in the Promised Land.

Understanding the life of Moses and the story of the children of Israel doesn't begin with the Book of Exodus. Rather, it begins at the end of the Book of Genesis, particularly Chapters 37–50. It is there that we

> The word *providence* is derived from the Latin prefix *pro*, which indicates "before or in front of." The root, *vidence*, comes from the Latin *videre*, meaning, "to see." So together, the word means, "to see beforehand." God sees what is needed beforehand and then provides.

read the story of Joseph, the beloved son of a man named Jacob. Thus, God's plan for Israel's freedom began before they were enslaved. As we read the final chapters of Genesis, we can see how God strategically places people where they need to be to accomplish God's will. So as sad and tragic as Joseph's story is as he was sold into slavery by his own brothers, we get hints that Joseph had to end up in Egypt to establish the context for Moses' life and purpose.

Once in Egypt, Joseph was sold to Potiphar, one of Pharaoh's officers and a captain of the guard (Genesis 37:36). From there, Joseph's life seemed to get worse. Potiphar's wife falsely accused Joseph of making sexual advances toward her, and he was put in prison. While imprisoned, Joseph correctly interpreted the dreams of two fellow prisoners, bringing him to the attention of Pharaoh, who was looking for someone to interpret his dreams. This course of events shows how

God's providence took Joseph from slavery to prison to Pharaoh's court to further God's plans.

Joseph interpreted Pharaoh's dreams, leading to his appointment as the king's second-in-command. From that position, he rose to the stellar heights of power and prestige and was placed in charge of storing provisions to carry Egypt through the coming famine.

When the famine arrived, Joseph's brothers went to Egypt to buy food. They dealt directly with Joseph, but because they didn't know about his exalted status, they didn't know who he was. Joseph eventually revealed himself to them, and they were reconciled. After a warm and moving family reunion, Joseph invited his brothers and his father to move to Egypt so they might enjoy plenty of grain and good land where they could raise crops and graze their flocks.

The pharaoh in power at the time responded to the arrival of Joseph's family favorably. He allowed Joseph and his family to settle in the fertile land of Goshen. They were given choice real estate in Egypt where they could live and raise their families in peace. For over 70 years after this radical relocation, life was good for Joseph and his family, but eventually all of that changed.

1. When have you sensed God's providence in your life?

2. What was your reaction?

3. Where did God's providence take you?

Problems

The last verse in the Book of Genesis says that Joseph died at 110 years old and was embalmed and placed in a coffin in Egypt. In the first chapter of the Book of Exodus, we read that around 70 of Jacob's family members originally entered Egypt, but the Israelites "multiplied greatly and became exceedingly numerous, so that the land was filled with them" (Exodus 1:6-7). Even after Joseph's death, the Israelites lived in peace and prosperity, and they continued to grow in number, to the dismay of the Egyptian officials.

Then, in verse 8, we read those ominous words: "Now a new king arose over Egypt, who did not know Joseph." The phrase "Now a new king" indicates that the story is about to take a turn; and the phrase "did not know Joseph" hints that it won't be a good turn. A new pharaoh sat on the throne after several centuries, and Joseph's name and reputation had become virtually unknown. This new king felt no sense of obligation to Joseph's descendants as did the former king, and he didn't know how Joseph had stepped out of obscurity and slavery to save the Egyptians from famine. That was ancient history, a bygone promise between a forgotten Joseph and a long-dead pharaoh.

The new king despised the growing Hebrew population. In fact, their growing numbers had become a problem. As long as they were a family of only 70 people, there was no need for the pharaoh to worry. But as the Israelites grew in number, they became a threat to the Egyptians. And with Joseph dead and no longer able to broker peace with the king, the Egyptians' attitude toward the children of Israel changed. They looked upon Israel with suspicion and fear. And as the world's bloody history shows us, mounting suspicion toward a group of people is only a step away from racism, another step away from persecution, and a stone's throw away from genocide.

Whether it is an Egyptian pharaoh, a Nazi Adolph Hitler, or a Ugandan Idi Amin, a tempting political strategy for new leaders is to solidify power by singling out a relatively weak minority or members of an outsider group and calling them the enemy. Although there is no hint in the biblical narrative that the Israelites were anything but faithful citizens of the empire, Pharaoh singled out the rapidly expanding Hebrew population as an emerging threat.

The delusional pharaoh imagined that the growing but still small Israelite minority in Egypt was more numerous and more powerful than his people. He warned the Egyptians that in the event of war, the

> Egyptian pharaohs were heads of state as well as religious leaders, "the divine intermediary between the gods and Egyptians." "The word *pharaoh* means, 'great house,' " a reference to the palace where he resided.[1]

> Joseph died in approximately 1805 BC, which would have coincided with the reign of Amenemhet III (1841–1797 BC). Though scholars have disagreed on who was the pharaoh in Moses' story, many scholars now believe that the pharaoh mentioned in the Book of Exodus is Ramses II.[2]

Israelites might join their enemies and fight against them. Pharaoh's comments will sound familiar to anyone who has studied American history. Each successive wave of immigration has triggered xenophobic concerns directed at Africans, Jews, the Irish, Asians, Latinos, and other ethnicities and religions.

Pharaoh tried three different strategies to stem the growth of the Israelite people. First, he enslaved them, thinking he could limit their growth by requiring them to do backbreaking work. He assumed that their strength as a people would decline in proportion to the adversity that they were required to bear. However, the opposite happened: The more they were oppressed, the more they multiplied and the stronger they grew (verse 12).

God has a unique way of using the trials in our lives to strengthen us if we trust God in and during what appears to be an unbearable process. The Israelites did not prosper because they were a superior people. They prospered because they worshiped a superior God.

Second, Pharaoh commanded the midwives to kill Hebrew boys at birth to keep them from growing up and becoming soldiers (verse 15). But Shiphrah and Puah, two brave midwives, refused to slaughter the babies. Pharaoh's cruelty was tragic and horrific for Israel, but it was also the providence of God as God was preparing the Israelites to be part of one of the most amazing comeback stories in human history. Although it didn't seem to be unfolding immediately, God had a plan for their eventual deliverance and freedom.

Just because bad things are happening to us and around us doesn't mean good things aren't happening through us. The good news is God has a plan for us, too. No matter how the pharaohs in our lives treat us, God is with us. And just as in the Israelites' case, God is working behind the scenes to turn cruelty and chaos into blessings and peace. God knows how, in God's time, to turn things around.

Third, Pharaoh ordered that all Hebrew baby boys be thrown into the river. However, one mother decided to resist Pharaoh's commands and chose to place her faith in God. She did not allow her fear to keep her from saving the life of her son.

When we are fearful, our faith must rise above our fears. We are living in a time of change and unrest. The events of our present time look as though they can't be solved or healed. Thus, there is no more appropriate time for us to put our faith and trust in God, despite our apprehensions. Our current fears are a perfectly normal response. However, this is why we must strengthen our faith. And the amount of our faith is not what is important; rather, it is the focus or object of our faith that is paramount.

1. What is the toughest problem you've ever faced?

2. Did you trust yourself to figure it out, or did you put faith in God to solve it?

3. How can you show courage and faith in the midst of chaos?

Say Their Names

Two midwives, Shiphrah and Puah, feared God more than they feared Pharaoh and refused to obey his commands. This move could have cost them their lives; however, they are known today for their courage and obedience to God. In fact, that we know the names *Shiphrah* and *Puah* is important. Not many women's names are mentioned in the Hebrew Bible, and when they are, they tend to be the names of queens. But aside from Moses' name, which appears at the end of our Scripture passage, Shiphrah's and Puah's names are the only ones mentioned in this text.

It seems that the names of the pharaoh ruling at that time, the names of the ruthless Egyptian taskmasters, and the names of the Egyptian masses who oppressed and killed the Hebrews have been lost to the dustbin of history. But it's as if the author of Exodus is shouting to us today, "Say their names! Do not forget Shiphrah and Puah, the midwives who feared God, outwitted the king, and saved Moses' life." Shiphrah and Puah said no to the powers of injustice and yes to life. They put themselves at great personal risk but turned the tables on fear and power. For those reasons, their names must not be forgotten.

1. What are the names of people who have played a major role in your life or mentored you in the faith?

2. What did they do that was pivotal or life-changing for you?

3. Think of people whose names you might have forgotten (teachers, pastors, coworkers, neighbors). Lift up to God as many names as you can remember, and say a prayer of thanksgiving for them.

Promise

Despite Pharaoh's cruel plans to destroy the Hebrews, God saved one baby who would be the future liberator of the children of Israel. Exodus 2:1-4 introduces us to Moses and his family: "A man from the house of Levi went and married a Levite woman. The woman conceived and bore a son. . . . When she could hide him no longer, she got a papyrus basket for him . . . and placed it among the reeds on the bank of the river. His sister stood at a distance, to see what would happen to him." (Note, our Scripture passage for this lesson doesn't name Moses' parents, Amram and Jochebed. Their names aren't mentioned until Exodus 6:20; and Miriam, Moses' sister, isn't named until Exodus 15:20. The writer of Exodus doesn't even mention Moses' name until the last verse of our passage [Exodus 2:10]).

During a time when many Israelites had become idolatrous, Moses' parents, Amram and Jochebed, were strong in their faith. Perhaps when they heard the Egyptian soldiers approaching, they thought the worse was about to happen. No doubt they flinched every time their baby cried because it meant that he might be discovered by the soldiers. They probably took careful pains to keep him quiet and out of sight.

If we want our faith to rise above our fears, we—like Amram and Jochebed—must put our faith in God. Only God is strong enough to move us and the world from its present state of unrest. Faith in God will help us through the storms of life, protect us in times of extreme danger, supply us with whatever strength we need, and guide us through our difficult seasons. Although our enemies may appear to be much larger, stronger, and better equipped, faith in God will give us victory over our enemies.

Amram and Jochebed knew that their newborn baby's life was in danger, but they also believed that God had a plan for him. Both parents placed their faith and trust in God (Hebrews 11:23), but our Scripture passage for this lesson focuses on Jochebed. Although she is mentioned only twice by name in the Bible (Exodus 6:20; Numbers 26:59), she has a lasting place as one of the immortal mothers of Israel. Even though the consequences for rebellion would have been harsh, she refused to throw away her child, no matter what edicts Pharaoh sent down.

Jochebed hid Moses for three months (Exodus 2:2). If anyone had found out she was hiding Moses, the Egyptians would have killed him and perhaps the whole family. So, when Jochebed could no longer safely hide her baby, she designed a waterproof bassinet, placed Moses in it, and placed both on the river, hoping that somehow he would survive.

Perhaps Jochebed remembered the story of Noah and how he built an ark and covered it with pitch inside and out. In the original Hebrew, Moses was not put inside a "basket" but rather inside an "ark," the same concept as in the story of Noah (Genesis 6–10). One of the more interesting interpretations suggests that an ark, unlike a ship or a boat, has no ability to determine the way it goes. The inability to navigate or chart a course means an ark is dependent completely on divine providence to reach its destination.

This is one of the things Noah's ark and Moses' ark (or "basket") had in common: Both were guided by divine providence to mark the beginning of a new phase in history. Jochebed believed she was placing her baby in God's care and protecting him from death. This courageous mother believed that God would save once again with an ark.

Midwives Shiphrah and Puah and Moses' mother, Jochebed, demonstrate that the practice of caring for and protecting children is paramount to preserving a people's culture. Black mothers have had a legacy of protecting their children or the children of others for centuries. This practice has its roots in Africa. But as African mothers were enslaved and brought to the Americas, they were prohibited from adequately caring for their children, whose well-being was left in the hands of slave masters for profit.

Unfortunately, many Black women still face injustices that keep them from fulfilling their role as mothers. There are "pharaohs" that make it difficult for Black women to receive access to affordable health care or quality education for themselves and their children. They also struggle with food insecurity and high rates of unemployment or underemployment. This is when the brave Jochebeds, Shiphrahs, and Puahs of our time need to stand up and speak out on behalf of those who can't do so for themselves.

Once Moses was afloat in his protective ark, it took the actions of two other courageous people to assure his safety. The first person was Moses' sister, Miriam. Jochebed sent her to keep a watchful eye on the baby as the river carried him farther from home. Though she was a child, Miriam exhibited great faith in protecting her brother.

The second person was Pharaoh's daughter. In God's providence, Pharaoh's daughter went down to the river at just the right time to discover Moses. Prompted by God, she responded to this special baby. She knew what would happen to him if she did not intervene and save him. Perhaps she also had tremendous compassion for the crying child who was all alone on the river. Thus, she showed a much gentler nature to that of her father.

Since she was aware of the baby's heritage, Pharaoh's daughter knew it would be best to find a Hebrew nurse for him. She could have hired an army of Egyptian nurses and nannies to take care of Moses, but God's providence guided her, though unknowingly, to give Moses back to his mother to nurse and care for him.

One can only imagine the fear in her heart as Pharaoh's daughter prepared to take Moses home to her father. She knew Pharaoh's edicts against the Hebrew people and couldn't have thought he would be pleased that she was adopting a boy born of the people he was oppressing. But she demonstrated how courageous and determined she was.

With her father's blessing, she raised Moses and provided him with the finest education Egypt had to offer. He studied geography, history, music, law, mathematics, writing, literature, and philosophy. This education would serve Moses well when he later wrote the Torah. Pharaoh's daughter groomed Moses to be a future leader, inadvertently giving him the tools he would need to lead the children of Israel out of slavery. While Moses was receiving the benefits of an Egyptian upbringing, Moses' mother was also teaching him about Yahweh.

Shiphrah, Puah, Jochebed, Miriam, and Pharaoh's daughter had no way of knowing that their acts of resistance would pay off. The midwives helped preserve the Hebrew people, Moses' mother and sister hid him and then trusted God to finish his journey, and Pharaoh's daughter positioned him in Egypt so that he could fulfill the destiny of leading God's people out of slavery to the threshold of the Promised Land. We can celebrate that the most important story in the Hebrew Bible and God's promise for God's people involves women shaping and determining events.

This is a testament that God often uses the weak and lowly to overcome the strong and mighty. Today, God's providence still includes women who act courageously, defy oppression, and are resourceful in tough situations. Many of these women have protected and cared for us, blazed trails, and played pivotal roles in our lives.

Jochebed might have woven that basket, fitted its lid, and sealed it with the waterproofing bitumen, but in her heart, she might have still been afraid of what might have happened to Moses once she let go of that basket. No matter how slyly she had researched the visits of Pharaoh's daughter to the river or coached Miriam's reactions, perhaps Jochebed thought rejection, betrayal, and death would be the result of her rebellion to Pharaoh's commands. Jochebed couldn't rely on her basket-weaving skills nor the compassion of Pharaoh's daughter. She could only rely on God to take care of her baby and take him to safety.

Photo: Egyptian Basket. Well-Preserved Egyptian Basket (c. 1480 bc), probably comparable to the one described as carrying Moses (Rogers Fund, 1936).

1. What promises has God made to you?

2. Have they been fulfilled? If so, how?

3. How has God's providence worked to lead you to God's promises?

Reflect and Pray

Paul said, "And we know that all things work together for good to them that love God, to them who are the called according to his purpose" (Romans 8:28). He didn't say all things are good. Rather, he said that God can make all things work together for good.

There are times when life feels as if it is out of control. Another racist act is reported. The test comes back positive, bringing with it our greatest fear. Someone we love dies unexpectantly, our long-term marriage or relationship crumbles, or we have one of those periods where nothing seems to go as planned. It is during these times that life seems arbitrary and unpredictable. It's in times like this that we need to increase and strengthen our faith in God's providence.

Everything that happened in Moses' story was according to God's perfect planning. Even Pharaoh's cruelty to the Hebrew people couldn't delay what God had in store for them. Through God's *providence*, God made everything happen in God's time and in God's way. And although Pharaoh created *problems* and tried to stop God's plan, the *promise* still came to pass. God raised up a leader and a liberator in Moses, who was saved by several women who obeyed God's leading.

God is always at work in our lives, even in the worst circumstances. We may become frustrated because God's providence doesn't answer every one of our questions, it doesn't make our problems go away, and it doesn't always lead us down an easy road. Instead, God's providence reminds us that God is in control, has a plan for our lives, and is designing beauty out of chaos.

Gracious God, help us to trust You in everything. Open our eyes to see Your providence and follow Your leading, even when we don't see where You're going or understand why. Strengthen our faith for the journey ahead. In Jesus' name. Amen.

---

[1] "Pharaohs," National Geographic Society, encyclopedic entry (nationalgeographic.org/encyclopedia/pharaohs/).

[2] "We May Now Know Which Pharaoh Challenged Moses," by Jean-Pierre Isbouts, *National Geographic* (December 28, 2018).

[3] "Well-Preserved Egyptian Basket" (c. 1480 bc), probably comparable to the one described as carrying Moses (Rogers Fund, 1936); public domain.

2

Lesson 2
Broken But Not Useless

Focus Scripture: Exodus 2:11-15–3:1-6

A Slave Revolt

Many slaves heard preachers talk about how Moses led the children of Israel out of slavery in Egypt to freedom in the Promised Land. Many of the slaves who heard this felt a deep connection to Moses' story. Their yearning for freedom and solidarity with the children of Israel can be heard in the strains of the negro spirituals "Go Down, Moses" and "O, Mary, Don't You Weep." While they had to do backbreaking work from sunup to sundown under their "pharaohs," the slave masters, they kept waiting and praying for their own Moses to lead them to freedom.

But for much of Moses' story, he wasn't exactly a hero or a savior. As a baby, he had to be rescued from certain death by several women who followed God's providence. And one unfortunate act made this middle-aged man flee his home in Egypt. He fled deep into the wilderness of a foreign land, where he shed all his Egyptian power and privilege for the nomadic lifestyle of a shepherd. Broken, rejected, and alone, it appeared that this might be Moses' final chapter. But that wasn't the case. Instead, God was positioning him to be used for something far greater than Moses could ever imagine!

In April 2020, the Black community lost a theological giant in the person of the Rev. Dr. Gayraud Wilmore, who at one time served as a pastor in West Chester, Pennsylvania, at Second Presbyterian Church of West Chester. In one of his many profound books, *Black Religion and Black Radicalism*, Dr. Wilmore highlights Nat Turner, an enslaved African American preacher in Virginia who led the bloodiest slave rebellion in American history.

Turner was born into slavery in Southampton County, Virginia. Between 1825 and 1830, he became a Baptist preacher to other enslaved people. His ability as a preacher and his personal charisma attracted a good number of followers. Opportunities were given to Turner that were denied others. He was taught how to read and write, and he listened to discussions on political and social issues from the most enlightened men and women in the country. But he grew weary of seeing his people suffering and dying at the hands of white slaveowners.

In 1825, he had a vision of a conflict between Black and White spirits. He also had a vision about a snake: "The Spirit instantly appeared to me and said the Serpent was loosened, and Christ had laid down the yoke he had borne for the sins of men and women, and that I should take it on and fight against the Serpent."[1]

Years later, Turner believed a solar eclipse was a signal from God that the time to rise up had come. On

> To learn more about Nat Turner and the 1831 Virginia slave revolt, watch the movie *The Birth of a Nation* (2016).

the night before he led the insurrection, he gave a speech to his followers in which he said that God had appointed that night for the Black race to be delivered from slavery and that war should be waged on a Christian basis. The bloody revolt began in the early morning hours of August 21, 1831. Turner and his followers led a series of attacks, going from house to house killing men, women, and children, beginning with his master's household. Most sources say that about 55 people were killed in Turner's slave rebellion.[2]

For some, Turner is considered a hero, a prophet, and a deliverer. For others, he is a villain. Because of his bloody insurrection, his place in history has been reinterpreted, revised, maximized, and minimized. His legacy is still debated, but before we condemn Turner for the people he killed, remember that he received his theology from the same place slave masters used to justify their evil oppression of enslaved people: the Bible. Turner said he was inspired by Moses, who had many things in common with Turner. Both men were broken by the lack of justice around them, but they were not useless.

Other similarities Moses and Turner shared: They were educated men who were given signs from God. They were inspired to rebel against the hierarchies of their time to lead their people out of enslavement. And they incorporated death into their fight for freedom. This is not to justify the taking of another person's life; we don't have that right. However, oppression can cause so much pain in people's lives that they may do the unjustifiable, causing them to feel broken. But God can work through those who are broken and allow them to be useful for the Kingdom.

1. Do you think Nat Turner's revolt was justified? Why or why not?

2. What might Turner's revolt against slavery have in common with Moses and the children of Israel's exodus out of slavery in Egypt?

3. How did Turner's brokenness move him to stand against injustice?

Broken

The Bible indicates that there are three significant periods in Moses' life, each one being 40 years. When we're first introduced to Moses in Scripture, he is a baby whose life is in danger because of Pharaoh's desire to kill all Hebrew baby boys to stop the growing numbers of the Hebrews. But the newborn Moses was rescued by the very household that had sent the edict for his death.

Later, according to Acts 7:22, Moses was instructed in all the wisdom of the Egyptians and was powerful in his words and deeds. We can also learn something about the first 40 years of Moses' life from the writings of an Egyptian called Manetho; the writings of the Jewish historian Josephus; or from Eusebius, a historian of the early church.

Josephus wrote that because Pharaoh had no son and heir, when Moses was brought to the palace by Pharaoh's daughter, Pharaoh began nurturing Moses for the throne. Being raised in the palace, Moses received a first-class education. He knew how to read and write in Egyptian hieroglyphs; he was taught the trade language of that period, Akkadian; and he would learn Hebrew from his mother, Jochebed. He was also well-trained in linguistics, mathematics, astronomy, architecture, music, medicine, philosophy, law, and the fine art of diplomacy. He was enjoying a life of the highest privilege, wealth, education, and comfort.

However, none of these things would have happened without God overruling Pharaoh's deadly decree. Everything that happened to Moses was part of God's divine plan. Moses was 40 years old at this point in our text, and his life was about to take a momentous turn.

All the years Moses had spent in Pharaoh's palace had not eclipsed his knowledge of his origins. Even though he lived in the affluence of the power that surrounded him, Moses seemed to have kept in touch with his roots. He knew who he was, and he knew who his people were.

Perhaps Jochebed had told him about his miraculous deliverance by the hand of God. By now, she would have taught him about God's sovereignty and providence, about the patriarchs and matriarchs (Abraham, Sarah, Isaac, Jacob, and Rebekah) and about God's revelation and promises to them. So, when Moses saw one of his Hebrew brethren being mistreated, he stepped in: "One day, after Moses had grown up, he went out to his people and saw their forced labor. He saw an Egyptian beating a Hebrew, one of his kinsfolk. He looked this way and that, and seeing no one he killed the Egyptian and hid him in the sand" (verses 11-12).

At some point in Moses' journey to adulthood, he became burdened over the plight of his people, the Israelites. A casual reading of verse 11 could make us think that Moses accidentally discovered the oppression of the Israelites. But there are clues in this text as to what Moses was thinking.

The phrase "his kinsfolk" is better translated "his people." Verse 11 says, "He went out to his people" and "one of his kinsfolk." Moses was identifying himself

> If Moses had been on trial for killing the Egyptian, a lawyer could have defended him based on the ancient legal principle *lex talionis* (lex-tally-OWN-nis), or the "law of retaliation." Theologian Philip Ryken argues that *lex talionis* is recorded in Exodus 21:23–25, which says, "If there is harm, then one shall pay life for life, eye for eye, tooth for tooth, hand for hand, foot for foot, burn for burn, wound for wound, stripe for stripe." Using this defense, Ryken states, "It could be argued that the Egyptian got exactly what he deserved."[4]

not as an Egyptian, but as an Israelite. The phrase "saw their forced labor" (or as one translation puts it, "looked on their burden") means, "to see with emotional distress," and it has a strong emotional overtone. Moses shared God's heart for God's people. Moses saw what was happening to them, and he could not take it any longer.

Some scholars argue that Moses "looked this way and that way" to ascertain that no one was watching him or would see that he was about to commit a crime. However, Moses should get the benefit of the doubt. Maybe he was looking around for someone to come and help the Hebrew man who was being beaten. From that perspective, Moses was looking to see if anybody would intervene or if they were just going to stand by and watch the Egyptian oppressor ultimately kill the Hebrew slave.

When no one seemed to be stepping up to defend the man, Moses intervened. We don't know if initially Moses was trying to break up the fight and the situation got out of control or if, in anger, he took matters into his own hands. Whatever the intention, the Egyptian died at Moses' hand, and Moses hid him in the sand. Many commentators accuse Moses of murder. However, Christian commentators such as Tertullian, a North African theologian from the late second and early third centuries, and Thomas Aquinas, a philosopher during the scholastic period, sought to clear Moses from the charge of murder.

The Hebrew language does not distinguish between the words *beating* and *killing*; the verb *nakah* refers to both. Thus, the word used to describe what the Egyptian did to the Hebrew and what Moses did to the Egyptian are one and the same. This suggests that the Egyptian intended to beat the enslaved Hebrew to death. If so, it could be argued that Moses did what he had to do to save a life, so perhaps he did not intend to kill the Egyptian. Thus, could this have been a simple case of retaliation—an eye for an eye and a wound for a wound? The Scripture text doesn't give us enough information for us to know for sure.

What we do know is that Moses committed a deadly action. How would this turn of events effect God's providence in Moses' life? Would Moses' actions that day break him and delay his destiny? Despite his years of privilege in Pharaoh's palace, why would Moses risk it all to help a people with whom he shared a heritage but not a culture?

Moses knew about the injustices pressed upon his people. Like Nat Turner, Moses could no longer wait for something to happen or for someone else to do something. The day came when resentment evolved into anger and injustice could no longer be ignored. Turner also felt that rage when he organized the slave revolt. He had watched his people be beaten, lynched, castrated, and raped while facing one injustice after another, so he could identify with Moses yearning to do something—anything—to set his people free.

Nevertheless, no matter how well-intended Moses might have been, his actions stand as a warning against allowing anger to go too far, even in the cause of justice. Moses' heroic rescue of the Hebrew slave is overshadowed by the death of the Egyptian slave master. Although most early Jewish literature lacks any negative judgment concerning Moses' act, in Christian tradition, Moses is often remembered as a murderer rather than a rescuer; however, Moses was a rescuer.

As Christians, we are permitted to become angry, but we are not supposed to allow that anger to turn to sin. Understandably, in the midst of all the injustices we see in our world, it's difficult to control our anger and indignation; but we cannot appoint ourselves as judge, jury, and executioner. If we do, we might lose the very victories we've fought so hard to win.

Moses learned that lesson soon after the death of the slave master: "When Moses went out the next day, he saw two Hebrews fighting; and he said to the one who was in the wrong, 'Why do you strike your fellow Hebrew?' He answered, 'Who made you a ruler and judge over us? Do you mean to kill me as you killed the Egyptian?' Then Moses was afraid and thought, 'Surely the thing is known'" (verse 13).

Because of Moses' actions the day before, news had spread among the Hebrews. But instead of lauding him as a hero, his own people had no respect for him and scorned him as a murderer. If we didn't know how Moses' story ends, it might be hard to believe that God could take Moses' mistake, his brokenness, and use it to save God's people.

Moses' actions caused Pharaoh to view Moses as a traitor who needed to be killed. But Moses "refused to be called the son of Pharaoh's daughter; Choosing rather to suffer affliction with the people of God, than to enjoy the pleasures of sin for a season" (Hebrews 11:24-26). Scholar Rabbi Hillel is quoted as saying, "Moses easily could have stayed in the lap of Egyptian luxury in the palace. Instead, he showed a key lesson of leadership: one 'should share the burdens of others.' "[3]

In that one act of trying to bring about justice, Moses lost everything. He had burned all his bridges with Pharaoh and the powers of Egypt, but he couldn't find a home among his people because they wanted nothing to do with him. Now, he was a man on the run but with nowhere to go.

1. How did taking the life of the Egyptian damage Moses?

2. What brokenness have you experienced? How did you deal with it?

3. Where has that hurt and pain affected you?

Positioned to Be Used by God

Moses left Egypt seemingly having ruined his life beyond repair. He was a fugitive from Pharaoh, and he was a rejected man among the Hebrews. But God was not surprised by the turn of events that drove Moses away from the palace. Sometimes God moves us from one place to position us more advantageously so God's will can be fulfilled: "For I know the plans I have for you," declares the Lord, "plans to prosper you and not to harm you, plans to give you hope and a future" (Jeremiah 29:11).

However, at this point in his story, Moses didn't know that he could still be used by God. A broken man, all Moses saw was his failure, rejection, and frustration. And he took all of that with him as he fled from Pharaoh and settled in Midian. Midian was a barren wasteland and adequately reflected Moses' reduced circumstances. Once the adopted grandson of Pharaoh, now Moses was a nomad living with the Midianites in the wilderness.

God often gives us wilderness experiences to test, to teach, or to tempt; but we often mistake these seasons as God abandoning us. Instead of embracing our wilderness moments, we sometimes wallow in self-pity, sure that God is no longer at work in our lives. So, we try to escape our hurt and confusion by overworking, shopping for things we don't need, watching pornography, or over- or undereating. Some of us pick up drug and alcohol addictions. Still others of us paste on a smile and try to pretend everything is all right so our families, friends, and coworkers won't know how miserable we are.

The wilderness represents isolation; and when we are broken, the wilderness can be a valuable training ground for us. In the Bible, the wilderness was often the place where God prepared those he was going to use (Jacob, Moses, the children of Israel, Elijah, John the Baptist, Jesus). Haunted by his past, cut off from the rest of civilization, and reduced to the daily necessities of food and water, Moses was forced to throw himself on the mercy of God's providence.

During this second 40-year phase of his life, Moses married a Cushite woman named Zipporah and became a shepherd for his father-in-law, Jethro. He wasn't aware of it at the time, but being a shepherd was the perfect job for him to learn how to be a leader. God used this time of apparent insignificance to prepare Moses for the significant work of shepherding the children of Israel, the flock of God. God was positioning Moses to be of use as a leader, a liberator, and a prophet. But in the meantime, God healed and humbled him.

So as Moses led flocks of sheep in the wilderness, God was preparing him to return to Egypt and free God's people. Moses would have to be strong in the face of a liberated but impatient and complaining people. Little did he know that in the last phase of his life, when most people are at their weakest, God would position Moses to free the children of Israel from generations of injustice, slavery, and oppression.

God's work is often a mystery to us. Rather than using the younger, more powerful Moses of Egypt when he was in his prime, God decided to use the weakened 80-year-old Moses of Midian. Why? Because a broken Moses was a better Moses. God's plan was to use all that Moses had become to accomplish Israel's deliverance from slavery. Therefore, Moses had to be positioned in what seemed to be a barren wilderness in his advanced age so he couldn't take any credit for the victories he was about to win. Instead, God would get all the glory.

1. How has God used your brokenness for something greater?

2. Do you fear the wilderness? Why or why not?

3. Thinking back on your wilderness experiences, what do you think you've gained from them?

Burned But Not Consumed

If you review Exodus 1–2, you might notice that God's voice is not heard. So, Exodus 3 begins describing the day when God was going to break a 40-year silence.

That day probably started out for Moses just like any other day. Verse 1 tells us that he went to the backside of the desert to care for Jethro's sheep. This illustrates two things. First, Moses wasn't sitting around waiting for God to speak. He was busy with his work. It might not have been the most exciting and ambitious job he could have had, but he still worked. God often calls people who are already busy at work, not those who are daydreaming and waiting for God to move while they do nothing. The insignificance of Moses' job should encourage us because it proves we do not have to have an influential position to be of service to God. Elite positions are not qualifications for God's service, but faith and character are.

Second, God will often appear on a regular day while we're going about the most mundane tasks. Moses probably never suspected on that day he might have a life-changing encounter with God. Many of us might be waiting for flashes of lightning, loud thunderclaps, or a booming voice from heaven. We may think this is the only way to hear from God, but like the children of Israel, we might be frightened if God spoke to us this way (Exodus 20:18-19).

Although God has used (and still can use) any of these methods

Moses and the Burning Bush, German, medal, medalist: Hans Reinhart the Elder (1538) Rogers Fund, 1912.

Moses' experience with the burning bush is known as a "theophany." A theophany is a physical appearance of God to a human being. Several theophanies are recorded in the Old Testament, but all had one thing in common: No one who experienced a theophany saw God's face.

Theophanies usually marked a turning point in people's lives as God gave orders or told them what would happen in their future. When they realized they were talking with God, they were often struck with terror, hiding their faces, or shielding their eyes. But no one in Scripture had as many encounters with God through theophanies as Moses.

to speak to people, that's not how the prophet Elijah found God. First Kings 19:11-13 says that God was not in the wind, an earthquake, or a fire. Instead, Elijah discovered God in the still, small voice. If we're not paying attention unless we see a bombastic display of divine showmanship, we might miss God's voice.

Moses' destination that day was Mount Horeb (also known as Mount Sinai), the mountain of God. This important location was not only the place where Moses would receive his call from God, but it would also be the place where the Ten Commandments would be given to Moses, the ark of the covenant would be made, and where God would be revealed and God's holy laws given to God's people.

Verse 2 says, "There the angel of the Lord appeared to [Moses] in a flame of fire out of a bush; he looked, and the bush was blazing, yet it was not consumed."

Moses' ordinary day was suddenly transformed by an

extraordinary sight: a flaming bush that was burning but was not consumed. The angel of the Lord never spoke, but the voice of God spoke directly to Moses through the burning bush.

A bush catching on fire in the dry desert is not unusual. The bush mentioned in this passage, however, was different. It appeared to be on fire even though it was not burning up. It was not even charred; it just kept burning. Moses' curiosity was piqued, and he went over to investigate: "I must turn aside and look at this great sight, and see why the bush is not burned up" (verse 3).

Our "burning bushes" are those circumstances or events that interrupt life and grab our attention. They are not part of our plans, but they do demand a response from us. In verse 4, we see that Moses didn't ignore the amazing bush. He turned aside. And when God spoke, Moses answered. "When the Lord saw that he had turned aside to see, God called to him out of the bush, 'Moses, Moses!' And he said, 'Here I am.'"

The fact that God repeated Moses' name is significant. Many of us can remember when we were children and how our parents called us when they wanted our attention. If we heard our name called more than once, or if our parents called us by our first, middle, and last names, that was usually a warning that they weren't playing games and wanted us to respond immediately. Calling someone by repeating his or her name may be for emphasis, attention, affection, tasks, or warnings. However, throughout Scripture, God repeated the names of those God spoke with to elevate them to places of importance.

After Moses' response, God said, "Come no closer! Remove the sandals from your feet, for the place on which you are standing is holy ground." Removing one's sandals was an ancient practice when entering a holy place of divine presence. It was a sign of reverence. But there wasn't anything particularly special about the ground Moses was standing on. It probably looked no different than any other patch of ground nearby. More than likely it was sandy, arid soil with scattered rocks and desert plants. What made the ground holy was that God had chosen to be present there in an auditory way.

When God identified God's self as "the God of your father," God's may have been referring to Moses' biological father, Amram. If so, then God was saying that he was the same God who rescued Moses from the Nile River, the God who Moses' parents taught him to serve before he went to Pharaoh's court. Other manuscripts put the word "father" in the plural, "the God of your fathers," which would refer instead to Abraham, Isaac, and Jacob.

If we subscribe to the latter translation, this will give us a different perspective. When we take a closer look at these vaunted patriarchs (Abraham, Isaac, and Jacob), we discover that they were all deeply flawed men. They were liars and tricksters, schemers and dreamers. Nevertheless, by His grace, God entered a personal relationship with them and used them to do great things and transcend their flaws and mistakes. And that's a message of hope and redemption for us, no matter how broken we think we are.

1. How do you think you would have reacted to the appearance of a burning bush that was not consumed?

2. In what ways did God show his power to Moses through the burning bush?

3. In what small, quiet ways has God appeared to you? What did you do?

Reflect and Pray

If we look back on our lives, we may see that some of our worst moments were our greatest opportunities to learn and grow. God will often take the pain and brokenness we live through and allow us to glean more knowledge, wisdom, and discernment. It's in God's nature to give us "beauty for ashes" (Isaiah 61:3); and through God's grace, those who "sow in tears shall reap in joy" (Psalm 126:5).

We shouldn't flee the wilderness. Instead, we should let our wilderness experiences prepare and position us for something greater. God doesn't lead us to the wilderness in vain. If we don't leave the comfort of our Egypt, we will probably never experience the opportunities God uses to work on us and to train us for what is ahead. The Bible says, "We are his workmanship, created in Christ Jesus for good works, which God prepared beforehand" (Ephesians 2:10).

We shouldn't allow our mistakes to break us, haunt us, nor define us. Paul gives us hope when he wrote, "We are troubled on every side, yet not distressed; we are perplexed, but not in despair; persecuted, but not forsaken; cast down, but not destroyed."

Father, I bring my brokenness and fear before you now. Help me in my wilderness moments. As I walk, help me to heal, learn, and grow. Turn my chaos into beauty for Your glory, so that I may do Your will. In Jesus' name. Amen.

---

[1] *Midnight in America: Darkness, Sleep, and Dreams During the Civil War*, by Jonathan W. White (University of North Carolina Press, 2017); page 93.

[2] "Nat Turner's Rebellion (1831)," by Patrick H. Breen, Encyclopedia Virginia, Virginia Humanities (encyclopediavirginia.org/entries/turners-revolt-nat-1831/).

[3] "Moshe: Portrait of the Leader as a Young Man," by Bryna Jocheved Levy, *Torah of the Mothers: Contemporary Jewish Women Read Classical Jewish Texts*, by Ora Wiskind Elper and Susan Handleman (Urim Publications, 2006).

[4] *Exodus: Saved for God's Glory*, by Philip Graham Ryken, Preaching the Word series, edited by R. Kent Hughes (Crossway, 2016); pages 51-52.

3

Lesson 3
Go Down, Moses
Focus Scripture: Exodus 3:7-12; 4:10-17

Sorrow Songs

W. E. B. DuBois referred to spirituals as "sorrow songs" because they were "the music of an unhappy people, of the children of disappointment."[1] DuBois was fascinated by the tension between hope and despair, joy and sorrow, death and life, and the ability of an enslaved people to embrace such polarities through music. But DuBois also perceived something of beauty in spirituals. He believed that the enslaved

Fisk Jubilee Singers in London. This photograph was commissioned by Queen Victoria, who arranged for it to be sent to America as a "gift from England to Fisk."

The Fisk Jubilee Singers were founded in 1871 by Fisk University treasurer and music professor George L. White. The a cappella group began as a nine-member ensemble of students and was formed to earn money for the fiscally struggling university. At performances, they sang negro spirituals and pre-Civil War songs sung by slaves. They were named Jubilee Singers while on tour. Professor White saw how physically and emotionally drained they were, and "in a gesture of hope and encouragement, named them 'The Jubilee Singers,'" referring to the year of jubilee mentioned in Leviticus 25.[4]

sang about their troubles but not without the affirmation of life and hope. They sang about the suffering they endured and the God who would deliver them.

Many slaves could not read so they memorized the Bible stories they heard and translated them into song, such as "Joshua Fit (Fought) the Battle of Jericho" and "Didn't My Lord Deliver Daniel?" In the early nineteenth century, a group of enslaved Africans put the Hebrews' Exodus story to song and called it "Go Down, Moses."

Ethnomusicologist John Lovell credits "Go Down, Moses" with "filling every listener with a pervasive contempt for oppression and a resounding enthusiasm for freedom."[2] Moses telling Pharaoh, "God says, 'Let my people go'" is a potent narrative. Slaves and those who tried to liberate them—such as Nat Turner, Denmark Vesey, and Gabriel Prosser—gained hope and inspiration from the Hebrews' exodus. Their escape from the South to the North was imagined as a flight from Egypt, enslavement, and Pharaoh to freedom in the Promised Land. Harriet Tubman, a conductor on the Underground Railroad, would be celebrated as "the Black Moses."

Although the Bible doesn't tell us that the children of Israel sang anything similar to spirituals to musically illustrate their Exodus experiences as they journeyed from Egypt, we do know that the oral tradition was the primary way of passing down information and remembering historical events. Later, these oral stories of the Exodus found their way into the Psalter. Several psalms mention Moses and the Hebrews' flight from Egypt: Psalms 77; 78; 80; 81; 105; 106; 114; 135; 136. These psalms, similar to the negro spirituals, immortalized the songs of the struggle for freedom and hope.[3]

1. Go online and find the lyrics to several negro spirituals. Read through them. Which lyrics talk about the struggles of the enslaved? Which lyrics talk of hope?

2. Read Psalms 77; 78; 80; 81; 105; 106; 114; 135; 136. How have these psalms encouraged people long after the Exodus?

3. If you keep a journal or would like to try a writing exercise, think of your personal struggles and desire for hope. Then write a stanza or a psalm describing your own exodus.

Go Down, Moses
When Israel was in Egypt's land,
Let my people go.
Oppressed so hard they could not stand,
Let my people go.
Go down, Moses,
Way down in Egypt's land.
Tell old Pharaoh, Let my people go.

We may assume that because Moses had gone from being a prince to being a shepherd that he was unhappy with his life in Midian. But Exodus 2:21 says that Moses "was content to dwell" with Jethro. He even married Jethro's daughter Zipporah. Perhaps these may have been the happiest years of Moses' life up to that point. He no longer lived the double life of a member of Pharaoh's household but with a Hebrew heritage. Also, he was no longer on the run for taking the life of the Egyptian. So, in middle age, Moses had found a sense of peace and stability. But as he neared the third phase of his life, God was about to turn Moses' life upside down.

In Exodus 3, Moses is tending his father-in-law's sheep when God calls to him from a burning bush. Then, in verses 7-12, God speaks to Moses about an important assignment, one that would be monumental in size and scale. God made it clear that He was fully aware of the Hebrews' suffering in Egypt and was now ready to act on their behalf: "I have observed the misery of my people who are in Egypt; I have heard their cry on account of their taskmasters. Indeed, I know their sufferings. . . . The cry of the Israelites has now come to me; I have also seen how the Egyptians oppress them" (verses 7, 9).

As he heard God talk about the people's oppression, perhaps Moses wondered what any of that had to do with him. Why was God talking to him about what was going on in Egypt? Moses had left Egypt and all its troubles behind, including the enslaved Hebrews who were still toiling under Pharaoh's tyranny.

But God didn't leave Moses in suspense for too long. "I will send you to Pharaoh to bring my people, the Israelites, out of Egypt" (verse 10).

Once God said that Moses would play a pivotal role in the freedom of the Hebrews, Moses questioned why he would be the right man for the job: "Who am I that I should go to Pharaoh, and bring the Israelites out of Egypt?" (verse 11). In response to Moses' question, God could have said, "You are the one I've been preparing for this moment since the day you were born."

In some ways, Moses' question in verse 11 is rhetorical. It didn't require an answer because Moses was using the question to signal to God that he wasn't confident in his abilities to be the leader of God's people. He wanted to justify his desire to remain a shepherd

> The love that God has for Israel is illustrated in the Hebrew word *hesed*. Many biblical scholars define *hesed* as "God's loving kindness toward humankind" or "God's unconditional love and mercy toward His creation, including humankind." *Hesed* is a love that is so enduring that it persists beyond any sin, betrayal, or brokenness. It's not simply a feeling, but an action; and it intervenes on behalf of others and comes to their rescue, even to those who are undeserving.

and continue his contented lifestyle in the desert of Midian.

And this wasn't the end of Moses' excuses. In Chapter 4, he is still trying to turn down the mission. He tried to wriggle out of God's call because he failed to realize that God knew exactly who Moses was when he called him, and God wasn't going to accept any of Moses' excuses. God knew Moses long before the burning bush or before his time in Egypt. But in that moment, as Moses stood before the burning bush, God's foreknowledge and providence was of little comfort to Moses. He still probably thought this was an impossible mission.

In the *Mission: Impossible* television program and movies, a recorded voice gives the team their assignment by saying, "Your mission, should you choose to accept it . . ." And after giving details of the mission, the team is given a warning: "Should you or any of your IM Force be caught or killed, the Secretary will disavow any knowledge of your actions. . . .

Good luck." But when God gives us monumental missions, God doesn't work this way. First, God didn't ask Moses if he wanted to accept the mission of freeing the Hebrews from enslavement and oppression in Egypt. God plainly told Moses that he had been chosen to be the Hebrews' liberator.

Second, unlike the recorded voice in *Mission: Impossible*, God wouldn't abandon or disavow Moses when he had to face Pharaoh. God promised, "I will be with you; and this shall be the sign for you that it is I who sent you" (verse 12). Moses could be confident that he wouldn't be returning to Egypt alone or without the power of the Lord going before him.

Third, because of God's providence and His promise to be with Moses, freeing the Hebrews would not be an impossible mission. God didn't find out by accident about the Hebrews' oppression after over 430 years and then begin to make plans and strategies to rescue them. God knew of their oppression and of Pharaoh's abuse; but because of God's perfect timing, God waited to bring forth the right man at the right time who would be a liberator for His people.

Sometimes the purpose and plan God has for our lives is not immediately known. The Bible records the journeys of many people God positioned and used in His providence. Often, those men and women didn't see God's promises come to pass right away. They waited years on those divine promises, and in the meantime, God prepared them for what lay ahead. For example, it took over 25 years for Abram and Sarah to have their son Isaac. Joseph languished in prison for years before he was brought before Pharaoh and exalted to his position of power. It took over a decade for David to become king, and seven more years before he was king over the whole nation.

In verse 7 and at the end of verse 10, the two-fold reference to "my people" shows the personal love and concern God has for Israel. God's love for Israel was not established at the Red Sea as they escaped the Egyptians nor at Sinai when God's glory was revealed. God called Israel "my people" from the beginning because God loved them with an everlasting love, or *hesed*.

Because of God's omnipresence and omniscience, God knew exactly what was happening with the Hebrews as well as with Moses. This indicates for us that God is never too far removed to know what is going on in our lives. The psalmist described a God who is acutely aware of everything that concerns us (Psalm 139), and the Gospel writers Matthew and Luke wrote that even the hairs of our heads are numbered (Matthew 10:30; Luke 12:7).

Because God knew that Israel's situation was so dire that they couldn't deliver themselves, God had to raise up a leader, a liberator, that God could position and use to deliver them. Thus, God called Moses to be that leader. Although the 80-year-old Moses had grown comfortable as a husband and a shepherd in the barren desert of Midian, God's mission for Moses was meant to disrupt that comfort and change his occupation.

1. When have you watched God use unlikely people or circumstances to fulfill His will?

2. Have you thought you were one of those unlikely people? If so, why?

3. What seemingly impossible missions has God called you to undertake?

An Unlikely Leader

>The Lord told Moses what to do.
>Let my people go.
>To lead the Hebrew children through.
>Let my people go.
>Go down, Moses.
>Way down in Egypt's land.
>Tell old Pharaoh,
>Let my people go.

Moses' attempts to persuade God to let him out of the mission were in vain. Moses may have thought he was an unlikely leader and wouldn't be able to carry out such a tremendous assignment, but God had no such doubts. God had plenty of experience using unlikely people for His purposes.

Abram left his home and family to go to a place God didn't reveal to him until he was farther along in his journey (Genesis 12). Then when he and his wife, Sarah, were in their advanced age, Abram—now Abraham—were promised a son that would take Abraham from being a father to being a father of many nations (Genesis 15). This seemed impossible for a barren, elderly couple, but nothing is impossible with God.

The prophet Elijah stood against 450 prophets of Baal and did the impossible. He repaired the altar of the Lord that had been in disrepair. After putting the sacrifice on the altar, Elijah then drenched everything with water. The people observing the prophet's strange actions probably thought there was no way the altar would catch on fire. But Elijah prayed to God, and God's fire fell from heaven. Not only did that fire consume the sacrifice and the wood, but it also consumed the stones and lapped up all the water. God took the impossible and performed a miracle (1 Kings 18)!

God called a young virgin named Mary to be the mother of Jesus, the Son of God and the Savior of the world. Mary was betrothed to Joseph but not married to him; and for her to become pregnant would have caused immense shame for her and her family and for Joseph and his family. Not unlike Moses, Mary was also surprised by God's assignment. She even asked, "How shall this be, seeing I know not a man?" (Luke 1:34). But Mary was willing to take on this strange mission. She was also willing to endure the shame and the possibility of breaking her betrothal and being ostracized by her community to do God's will (Matthew 1).

God can do the same for us. God is aware of our faults, flaws, mistakes, and insecurities, but none of that can hinder God's will. In fact, God often uses the worst parts of us for God's glory. If we're willing to trust God, God will take the things about ourselves and the things we've done that we're ashamed of and use them to help us to carry out the assignment and to reach people for the Kingdom.

And when God prepares us for the mission, God always gives us the appropriate credentials. God promised to be with Moses, but God also gave Moses all the information he needed: "God said unto Moses, I AM THAT I AM: and he said, Thus shalt thou say unto the children of Israel, I AM hath sent me unto you" (Exodus 3:14).

Moses knew his own credibility in Egypt was gone after killing the Egyptian and being rejected by the Hebrews, so he was probably wondering how he was going to convince his people to follow him out of Egypt. But God told him that he would say, "I AM hath sent me unto you." God didn't give Moses special papers with an official seal, a card embossed with God's name and address, or God's résumé. God simply said, "I AM hath sent me unto you."

Bible commentator Terence Fretheim states that verse 14 is "one of the most puzzled over verses in the Hebrew Bible."[5] In Hebrew, the phrase "I AM" is spelled *YHWH*. In theological circles, it is known as the "tetragrammaton," the combination of four Hebrew letters to form the ancient Hebrew name of God, *YHWH*.

The name *YHWH* appears in the Torah and in every Hebrew Scripture, except for Esther and Song of Solomon. *YHWH* means "to be" or "to exist" or "to cause to become." We pronounce *YHWH* as "YAHweh," but it's a word that purposely has consonants without vowels because the Hebrew people believed that God's name was so sacred, so holy, the whole word shouldn't be written or pronounced.

Most intriguing, God's name is also a verb, which indicates that God is active, not static. God cannot be boxed in by definition or doctrine. As finite beings, we are limited, and we cannot conceive of an infinite and unlimited God. God cannot be limited by our labels. When God declared, "I AM who I AM," God was telling Moses—and by extension the Hebrews and us—that our God encompasses everything. It's the ultimate expression of God's total self-sufficiency, self-existence, and immediate presence.

God's "I AM" is whatever we need God to be whenever we need God to be. The children of Israel needed God to deliver them from oppression, and God—through Moses—would be that deliverer. And today, the struggle for freedom, equality, and justice is not over. We still need a Moses who will stand up to the modern pharaohs and declare God's supremacy and deliverance. God is not unaware of the racism, sexism, discrimination, sexual harassment and abuse, mass incarceration, unjust laws, and violence in our world. In God time, God will deliver God's people.

1. What does God's "I Am" mean to you?

2. What have you needed God to be to you in different circumstances?

3. How did God come through for you in those circumstances?

Excuses, Excuses

> No more shall they in bondage toil.
> Let my people go.
> Let them come out with Egypt's spoil.
> Let my people go.
> Your foes shall not before you stand.
> Let my people go.
> And you'll possess fair Canaan's land.
> Let my people go.
> Go down, Moses,
> Way down in Egypt's land.
> Tell old Pharaoh,
> Let my people go.

Exodus 4:10-17 continues a dialogue between God and Moses, with Moses continuing to make excuses to why he shouldn't return to Egypt and face Pharaoh, and God telling him exactly why he should. Moses

In the ancient Near East, leprosy was a dreaded disease with no known cure. Lepers were excluded from worship and made to live in perpetual quarantine in camps, loudly declaring their humiliation by crying, "Unclean! Unclean!" (Leviticus 13:45). When Moses witnessed God restoring his leprous hand, that was an amazing feat! Not only did God prove to Moses that He could do what was humanly impossible, this also symbolized that God could restore the children of Israel.

gave at least five objections or excuses, but given the magnitude of the assignment, it's not altogether unreasonable that Moses would be hesitant.

Moses was an 80-year-old fugitive, and God was calling him to confront the most powerful man in the world? In addition, Moses would then be responsible for removing almost two million enslaved Hebrews from Egypt, who depended on their cheap labor to regulate its economy. And these were Hebrews who had known no other home than Egypt and no other life than a life of enslavement. No wonder Moses objected!

But after each of Moses' excuses, God patiently answered and assured him. When Moses had given all his objections, it was clear to God that Moses simply did not want to go. Moses needed confirmation. In Chapter 3, God assured Moses that to be with him, but that didn't seem to suffice. So, in Exodus 4:10-17,

God counters each of Moses' excuses with even more assurances and reassurances.

Moses' fear of what the Hebrew people would say prompted him to give his first objection in Exodus 4:1: "Suppose they don't believe me or listen to me, but say, 'The LORD did not appear to you.'" God answered Moses with a question, "What is in your hand?" (verse 1). As a shepherd, Moses carried the tool of the trade, a shepherd's crook or staff. When Moses told God he was carrying a staff, God told him to throw the staff on the ground. Here, God showed Moses the first of many signs.

Moses' staff became a snake. Then when God instructed Moses to pick up the snake, it turned once again into a staff. Not only did this sign confirm God's power to Moses, but it showed that when yielded to God, the most common and mundane things can become powerful tools.

Then God performed a second sign. God told Moses to put his hand inside his cloak. When he pulled his hand out, Moses saw that it was white with leprosy. When he obeyed God by putting his hand back inside his cloak and pulling it out again, he saw that his hand had been healed.

As a final sign to Moses, God told him that if the people didn't believe him, he should take water out of the Nile River, pour it on dry ground, and it would become blood. The Nile was the life blood of Egypt, the main source of water for the crops. Turning that precious life source into blood would show that nothing and no one was beyond God's power.

God gave Moses these three signs to assure him that he would be accompanied by God when he returned to Egypt, and that neither Pharaoh's power nor the Hebrews' potential rejection of Moses was a match for God's providence. After this demonstration of God's power, Moses should have been out of excuses, but he had one more excuse.

"O my Lord, I have never been eloquent, neither in the past nor even now that you have spoken to your servant; but I am slow of speech and slow of tongue" (verse 10). This seems to be a strange excuse for a man who was given a world-class education in Egypt. He might have been roaming the desert as a shepherd when God called him, but he wasn't illiterate. Neither had he always lived as a nomad in the middle of nowhere. Moses was no stranger to the courts of power; and he was well-versed in many educational disciplines. How, then, could his speech have been a problem?

Whether Moses had a speech impediment, or another type of difficulty speaking, is not relevant. If Moses' speech was deficient, God knew that and had still called him, so that wasn't something Moses needed to worry about. And if Moses struggled with speaking, perhaps God wanted him because of this flaw. The Bible never says that God wanted someone who had perfect oratory skills. Perhaps God wanted Moses with all his flaws because he could be more relatable and accessible.

In response to Moses' concerns about his speech, whatever that might have been, God said, "Who gives speech to morals? Who makes them mute or deaf? . . . Is it not I the LORD? Now go, and I will be with your mouth and teach you what you are to speak" (verses 11-12). God used emphatic language to drive home to Moses that as the Creator and Sustainer of the universe, God could handle all obstacles in getting the Israelites out of Egypt.

If God wanted perfection, God could work through angels who are without sin and flaws. But despite—and sometimes because of—our foibles, God continuously decides to work through human beings. God works through broken, imperfect people to fulfill God's perfect will.

Paul said, "Consider your calling: not many of you were wise according to worldly standards, not many were powerful, not many were of noble birth. But God, God chose what is foolish in the world to shame the wise; God chose what is weak in the world to shame the strong; God chose what is low and despised in the world, even things that are not, to bring to nothing things that are, so that no human being might boast in the presence of God" (1 Corinthians 1:26-29).

After this conversation between God and Moses, excuses and objections didn't deter God and God's purposes. God promises to be with us, no matter what task God has given us; and if we yield our flaws to God, God will use them to achieve God's will.

1. Why do you think Moses gave God so many excuses for not wanting to take on the assignment of freeing the children of Israel?

2. What excuses have you given God for not wanting to obey His word or carry out His missions?

3. How has God assured you of His presence?

Reflect and Pray

The negro spirituals are part of the oral tradition of African Americans who composed and sang these sorrow songs as a reflection of their struggles and of their faith. When they heard sermons about Moses leading the children of Israel to freedom, enslaved Americans could closely identify with the bondage, oppression, and injustice of the Bible. We explore the spirituals today to remember our ancestors and to honor their desire to be free. But these songs also give us a unique perspective on the Exodus and Moses' role in being a liberator and a leader when all the odds were stacked against him.

When our tasks appear bigger than our abilities, or our flaws make us feel incapable to take on a seemingly impossible mission, God still calls us. And when God calls us, as with Moses, God uses our flaws and insecurities to do great and miraculous things.

And the Scripture passages for this lesson are clear that none of our excuses or objections are enough to make God change God's mind about us. But those excuses give us the opportunity to receive God's assurances and confirmation. If we trust God and God's presence with us, we can accomplish anything God's tells us to do.

Father, forgive me for all the times I've answered your call with a list of excuses. Forgive me for justifying my reluctance and insecurity. When I am weak and afraid, reassure me of Your divine presence. Strengthen my resolve to do your will without excuse. In Jesus' name. Amen.

---

[1] *The Souls of Black Folk*, by W. E. B. DuBois (Create Space Independent Publishing Platform, 2014); page 118.
[2] *A Study Guide for Anonymous's "Go Down, Moses,"* Gale, Cengage Learning (Gale Study Guides, 2017).
[3] "Psalm 114 as reinterpretation of the exodus during and after the exile," Old Testament Essays, Hendrik Bosman (Old Testament Society of South Africa, 2013).
[4] "Our History," Fisk Jubilee Singers (fiskjubileesingers.org/about-the-singers/our-history/).
[5] *Exodus: Interpretation: A Bible Commentary for Teaching and Preaching*, Terence E. Fretheim (Westminster John Knox Press, 2010); page 63.

4

Lesson 4

Let My People Go

Exodus 5:1-9; 20-23; 6:1-9

Aaron to the Rescue

For millions of people over the centuries, the Exodus has been a powerful metaphor for struggle, deliverance, hope, and freedom. But perhaps no group has felt more connected to the plight of the children of Israel in slavery than African Americans. Throughout our history, enslaved people as well as free men and women have preached, sung, written, and spoken on themes related to the Exodus and eventual freedom in the Promised Land.

The enslaved sang spirituals such as "O, Freedom" and "Go Down, Moses." Zora Neale Hurston wrote the novel *Moses, Man of the Mountain*. Reggae musician Bob Marley sang "Exodus," and poet Yakov Azriel wrote "Have You Heard About Moses? What's His Name?" Various other artists, musicians, writers, and preachers have cast African Americans in the role of Israelites, enslaved but chosen by God for a glorious new freedom.

God called Moses to go to Egypt and liberate over two million Hebrews who were enslaved under Pharaoh. This was a monumental task that Moses was not sure he could do. Even if he had been confident he could do it, he made it clear from all the excuses he made that he didn't have a desire to return to Egypt and engage with his people. In the last phase of his life, he seemed quite content to live with his family and roam the Midian desert with his father-in-law's sheep.

But God's plans superseded Moses' unwillingness to take on this mission. God wanted to deliver the children of Israel from slavery and lead them to a land of freedom that they could call their own. God decided that the man to lead them to safety would be the 80-year-old shepherd Moses. Now it was time for Moses to start his journey back to Egypt and deliver a profound message to Pharaoh: "Thus says the Lord, the God of Israel, 'Let my people go' " (Exodus 5:1).

Moses told God that one of the reasons he wasn't up to the task of confronting Pharaoh was because he was "slow of speech and slow of tongue" (Exodus 4:10). He may have been referring to a speech impediment, or perhaps he stuttered. The Bible isn't clear about what Moses meant. But God had no plans to reverse the call to Moses because Moses may not have been able to speak clearly.

Instead, God recruited Moses' brother, Aaron, to serve as a spokesman. "What of your brother Aaron the Levite? I know that he can speak fluently; . . . You shall speak to him and put the words in his mouth; and I will be with your mouth and with his mouth, and will teach you what you shall do. He indeed shall speak for you to the people; he shall serve as a mouth for you, and you shall serve as God for him" (Exodus 4:14-16).

With God anointing Aaron to speak for Moses, there were no excuses left. God had thought of everything and had planned this mission down to the smallest details. Moses had two final things to do before facing off with Pharaoh. First, he wanted to talk with Jethro, his father-in-law, and ask him for permission to leave Midian and return to Egypt (Exodus 4:18). Second, Moses needed to meet with Aaron and tell him everything God had said at the burning bush (Exodus 4:28).

But before Moses met with Aaron, God gave him one final assurance. "Go back to Egypt; for all those who were seeking your life are dead" (Exodus 4:19). Most biblical scholars debate who the pharaohs were during Moses' lifetime; but many agree that the pharaoh on the throne when Moses fled Egypt was probably Seti I, and the pharaoh ruling at the time of the Exodus was Ramses II.[1] The pharaoh of his youth and anyone else who had wanted Moses to be punished for killing the Egyptian—they were all dead, so Moses could return to Egypt without fear of retribution or punishment.

Even before Moses and Aaron reached Egypt, Aaron had his first opportunity to speak for his brother. "Moses and Aaron went and assembled all the elders of the Israelites. Aaron spoke all the words that the LORD had spoken to Moses, and performed the signs in the sight of the people. The people believed;

and when they heard that the Lord had given heed to the Israelites and that he had seen their misery, they bowed down and worshiped" (Exodus 4:29-31). There was nothing left to do but for Moses and Aaron to deliver God's message to Pharaoh: "Let my people go."

1. Who has God assigned to come alongside to help or rescue you?

2. How has your ministry been enriched by their presence?

3. God told Moses that all the people who had wanted to punish him were dead. In other words, his past in Egypt was no longer a hindrance to him fulfilling his mission. Have you allowed your past to stop you? If so, how can you let your past die so it will no longer hinder you?

Audience with Ramses II

Statue of Ramses II, Luxor Temple, Egypt.

The Showdown

God's message to Pharaoh, "Let my people go," has been a rallying cry for many leaders who have led revolts and resistance movements against oppressors. Enslaved leaders such as Toussaint L'Ouverture, Nat Turner, Denmark Vesey, and Gabriel Prosser uttered this directive to the pharaohs of their day. But for Moses, there was more to the message.

God instructed Moses to tell Pharaoh to let the children of Israel go so they could "celebrate a festival to [God] in the wilderness" (Exodus 5:1). Given the customs of the ancient Near East, this request was not unreasonable. During that period, every nation presented sacrifices to its deities and celebrated festivals in their honor. Each culture had its own modes of worship, which were supposed to be appointed by the gods themselves. But when Moses delivered God's message, Pharaoh said no.

Why would Pharaoh refuse to obey God's message through Moses? First, God had already warned Moses that Pharaoh was going to say no: "When you go back to Egypt, see that you perform before Pharaoh all the wonders that I have put in your power; but I will harden his heart, so that he will not let the people go" (Exodus 4:21). So, neither God nor Moses was surprised by Pharaoh's response.

Second, though the people being allowed to worship God in the wilderness wasn't an unreasonable request, Pharaoh was not ignorent. If he allowed that many of the Hebrews to get too far from their work for any length of time, what would guarantee that they would return? Escaped slaves would devastate the Egyptian economy, which benefited from their cheap labor.

Third, the ruling pharaoh, Ramses II, was considered to be a god in human form, so he "was not accustomed to taking orders from lesser gods, let alone an unknown like Yahweh. 'Who is the Lord,' he inquired, 'that I should heed his voice and let Israel go? I do not know the Lord, and moreover I will not let Israel go.' Thus, the stage was set for a long struggle between a distrustful ruler with an outsize ego and a prophet with a new understanding of Yahweh and his power."[2]

Moses was not deterred. He came back with a modified proposal: "The God of the Hebrews has revealed himself to us; let us go a three days' journey into the wilderness to sacrifice to the Lord our God, or he will fall upon us with pestilence or sword" (verse 3). But Moses' new request only served to make Pharaoh angrier, and the enslaved Hebrews would pay the price!

Pharaoh was so infuriated by Moses' request that he commanded the taskmasters as well as their supervisors not to provide the Hebrews with straw to make bricks. Instead, they would have to gather the straw themselves but still make the same quantity of bricks they had always made. Pharaoh had just doubled the workload for the Hebrews, and it was all thanks to Moses. Once the Hebrews heard that Pharaoh had increased their already backbreaking labor, they were understandably angry.

Straw was an essential ingredient to making bricks because it reinforced the clay and helped the bricks stay intact. Although Egyptian temples were generally made of stone, their palaces, storehouses, administrative buildings, and official residents were all made of bricks. Thus, it took millions of bricks to satisfy the architectural ambitions of the pharaohs, and now because of Moses' request, the children of Israel were being forced to gather their own straw or try to make bricks without straw.

Because they were not able to gather the straw they needed, the Hebrews had to use stubble, which was an inferior substitute for straw. It's the part of the plant that remains in the ground after cereal grasses are harvested. Stubble is good for soil retention, but it isn't good for food or for brickmaking. It didn't hold the bricks together, which meant production slowed, and not as many bricks were being made, so the Hebrews weren't meeting their quota. Because of this, the taskmasters beat the workers more.

To add to the enslaved Hebrews' hardship, they had to work under brutal conditions. "They worked out in the hot Egyptian sun all day (often in temperatures over 100 [degrees]), driven to optimum production by taskmasters. They had no hats to protect their heads and wore nothing but a brief kilt or apron on their bodies." The intense heat affected their kidneys, the rough work making bricks tore the skin on their hands, and their lack of water as they worked made them regularly dehydrated. Not surprisingly, many of the Hebrews died "of dehydration, heat prostration, [and] heatstroke."[3]

The enslaved Hebrews had held out high hopes and had trusted Moses to persuade Pharaoh to allow them to leave. But now those hopes had been dashed. Not only were they not going to be allowed to leave, but their work had been made even more difficult. It's at times like these when the oppressed look for someone to blame. They needed a scapegoat on which to place all their anger, and Moses was the perfect target. They saw Moses' confrontation with Pharaoh as an enormous failure, which had resulted in their increased hardship and anguish. "The Lord look upon you and judge! You have brought us into bad odor with Pharaoh and his officials, and have put a sword in their hand to kill us" (verse 21).

This scene is reminiscent of earlier in Moses' life, before he fled Egypt, when he had tried to help his fellow Hebrews. "When he went out [the day after killing the Egyptian], he saw two Hebrews fighting; and he said to the one who was in the wrong, 'Why do you strike your fellow Hebrew?' He answered, 'Who made you a ruler and judge over us? Do you mean to kill me as you killed the Egyptian?'" (Exodus 2:13-14). Now, after confronting Pharaoh on behalf of the Hebrews, once again they rejected Moses.

Many of us know how Moses must have felt. Doing the right thing is not a guarantee of popularity, acceptance, or approval. People who have acted for the most righteous of reasons have been misjudged, blamed, rejected, and persecuted. Under those circumstances, it's extremely difficult to change hearts and minds and persuade people to see what we see, to risk everything to fight injustice and inequality.

So, the Hebrews blamed Moses, and in frustration, Moses blamed God: "O Lord, why have you mistreated this people? Why did you ever send me? Since I first came to Pharaoh to speak in your name, he has mistreated this people, and you have done nothing at all to deliver your people" (Exodus 5:22-23).

Like Moses, we are guilty of blaming God, too. When we believe we're on the right path and have done God's will, but things don't work out the way we envisioned them, our knee-jerk reaction is to blame someone. Often, that someone ends up being God. We want someone to take the blame for how things have gone sour and for how lost and confused we are. But that's when we need to remember God's promises and look to God word for reassurance. God is a promise-keeping God, but it's easy to forget that in the fog of doubt, anger, and hurt.

But God is gracious and merciful, even when we blame God needlessly. God did not rebuke Moses for his shortsightedness or his forgetfulness of God's promises. Instead, God made it clear that this first showdown between Moses and Pharaoh was nothing compared to the main event God had planned. "Now you shall see what I will do to Pharaoh: Indeed, by a mighty hand he will let them go; by a mighty hand he will drive them out of his land" (Exodus 6:1). The best was yet to come!

1. When have you obeyed God's commands but still faced resistance, rejection, and blame?

2. Like Moses, did you then blame God for what happened? If so, why?

3. How did God respond?

Scholars debate which pharaohs ruled during different historical periods. But many scholars believe that Ramses II, or Ramses the Great, was the pharaoh when Moses and Aaron went to Egypt to deliver God's message: "Let my people go."

Ramses's father, Seti I, designated him as his successor when Ramses was a boy; Ramses was a captain of the army at ten years old. He was also made a regent, and he accompanied Seti on various campaigns. By the time Ramses came to power, he had extensive knowledge and experience of "kingship and war." Ramses II ruled from 1279 to 1213 bc, the second longest reign in Egyptian history. He was a popular ruler but was known for his ego, which was the catalyst for his "extensive building programs" and the many statues of him found in Egypt.

Not much is known about the personal life of Ramses. He had numerous wives, of which several were Hittite princesses, but Nefertari seems to have been his favorite queen. There is a temple and a tomb named for her. Like many rulers of his time, he had a rather large harem, and he fathered over 100 children.

Upon his death, Ramses was succeeded by his thirteenth son, Merneptah. Ramses' mummy is preserved at the Egyptian Museum in Cairo.[4]

A Promise-Keeping God

Although God had warned Moses that Pharaoh's heart would be hardened, Moses was still frustrated with the outcome. Not only had Pharaoh rejected Moses' request, but the ruler took out his anger on the enslaved Hebrews by increasing their workload. To make matters worse, when the Hebrews heard about what Pharaoh had done, they became angry and turned on Moses. Then Moses blamed God for everything that had happened.

In Exodus 6, God reassures Moses that the story is not over. Then God made five promises:

- **First Promise:** "I will free you from the burdens of the Egyptians and deliver you from slavery to them" (verse 6).
- **Second Promise:** "I will redeem you with an outstretched arm and with mighty acts of judgment" (verse 6).

- **Third Promise:** "I will take you as my people, and I will be your God" (verse 7).
- **Fourth Promise:** "I will bring you into the land that I swore to give to Abraham, Isaac, and Jacob" (verse 8).
- **Fifth Promise:** "I will give it to you for a possession. I am the LORD" (verse 8).

Sometimes we, too, need to be reminded that God keeps every promise made. It can be difficult to hold on to those promises when we witness so much abuse, injustice, and oppression in our world. And it seems when good people try to speak up and be a voice for the marginalized, they are disparaged. But God is faithful and will honor promises made.

It's not that God breaks God's promises, but often God wants to show God's power in bringing those promises to fruition. We might not appreciate God when circumstances are too easy. It's usually when God intervenes in miraculous and powerful ways that God is assured of getting the glory, and we're not tempted to claim it for ourselves.

Unfortunately, the children of Israel weren't ready to hear more about God's promises. Verse 9 says, "Moses told this to the Israelites; but they would not listen to Moses, because of their broken spirit and their cruel slavery." There's nothing like a setback to crush our dreams and break our spirits. Although the children of Israel should have trusted God, it's understandable why they would feel dejected after Moses' meeting with Pharaoh.

A people with a broken spirit become skeptical and cynical.

Writer Robert Alter translates the Hebrew word for "crushed or broken spirit" as *kitzer ruach*, or "shortness of breath."[5] A broken spirit is also like a cancer that affects everything else in life. It can negatively affect our minds and our bodies. We can become cynical and skeptical. After Pharaoh's cruel actions, the enslaved Hebrews probably wished that Moses had never met with the king. Before their confrontation, at least the work wasn't increased as it was when Pharaoh became angry with Moses.

That mentality allows people with a broken spirit to become comfortable in their slavery and oppression. "As bad as it was, at least things were better than they are now." The Hebrews would revert to this same cynical mindset many times on their journey to the Promised Land.

When we allow our brokenness to make us lose hope, we lose the will and the courage to act for change for a better future. But as Christians, it's reassuring to know that our faith is hope-based and hopeful. This is what grounds us in an intrinsic relationship with God and God's action. Our belief in Christ is not simply eschatological or futuristic. Our hope is an inaugurated eschatology. In other words, it is both "already" and "not yet."

This "already" and "not yet" recalls the ancient concept of *Sankofa*. The word *Sankofa* is derived from the Akan (ah-kaan) people of West Africa. Expressed in the Akan language, *Sankofa* means, "It is not taboo to go back and fetch what you forgot." The symbol of *Sankofa* is a mythic bird flying forward while looking back and holding an egg, which symbolizes the future. The bird, while flying forward, looks back to connect to the past to give birth to a more prosperous and hopeful future.

That future includes God's promises. The Bible gives us so many promises that God is ready and willing to keep, but we must believe in the promise-keeping God who is faithful to His word. When we're feeling hopeless, these are a few of the promises we can use to encourage us along our faith journey:

- **Joshua 1:9:** "This is my command—be strong and courageous! Do not be afraid or discouraged. For the Lord your God is with you wherever you go."

- **Psalm 23:4-6:** "Even though I walk through the darkest valley, I fear no evil; for you are with me; your rod and your staff—they comfort me. You prepare a table before me in the presence of my enemies; you anoint my head with oil; my cup overflows. Surely goodness and mercy shall follow me all the days of my life, and I shall dwell in the house of the Lord my whole life long."

- **Psalm 27:5:** "For he will hide me in his shelter in the day of trouble; he will conceal me under the cover of his tent; he will set me high on a rock."

- **Psalm 46:1:** "God is our refuge and strength, a very present help in trouble."

- **Isaiah 26:3:** "Those of steadfast mind you keep in peace—in peace because they trust in you."

- **Isaiah 40:31:** "Those who wait for the Lord shall renew their strength, they shall mount up with wings like eagles, they shall run and not be weary, they shall walk and not faint."

- **Isaiah 41:10:** "So do not fear, for I am with you, do not be dismayed, for I am your God. I will strengthen you and help you; I will uphold you with my righteous right hand."

- **Isaiah 43:2:** "When you pass through the waters, I will be with you; and through the rivers, they shall not overwhelm you; when you walk through fire you shall not be burned, and the flame shall not consume you."

- **Isaiah 54:10:** "Though the mountains be shaken and the hills be removed, yet my unfailing love [kindness] for you will not be shaken nor my covenant of peace be removed, says the Lord, who has compassion on you."

- **Isaiah 54:17:** "No weapon that is fashioned against you shall prosper, and you shall confute every tongue that rises against you in judgment. This is the heritage of the servants of the Lord and their vindication from me, says the Lord."

- **Jeremiah 29:11:** " 'For I know the plans I have for you,' says the Lord. 'They are plans for good and not for disaster, to give you a future and a hope.' "

- **John 10:10:** "The thief comes only to steal and kill and destroy. I came that they may have life and have it abundantly."

- **John 14:16, 26:** "And I will ask the Father, and he will give you another Advocate, to be with you forever. . . . But the Advocate, the Holy Spirit, whom the Father will send in my name, will teach you everything, and remind you of all that I have said to you."

- **Hebrews 10:23:** "Let us hold unswervingly to the hope we profess, for he who promised is faithful."

- **Hebrews 13:5:** "Keep your lives free from the love of money, and be content with what you have; for he has said, 'I will never leave you or forsake you.' "

- **James 1:5:** "If any of you lacks wisdom, you should ask God, who gives generously to all without finding fault, and it will be given to you."

1. Using the concept of Sankofa, how can you look back to your past to help you move forward into your future?

2. Have you ever lived through an experience that broke your spirit? How were your thoughts and decisions different than when you are healed and whole?

3. Read through the list of biblical promises. Which ones are relevant for your current circumstances?

Reflect and Pray

As African Americans look back to Moses, the Exodus, and the children of Israel, we find a God who looks out for the oppressed, the enslaved, the disadvantaged, the marginalized, and the voiceless. We also find a promise-keeping God who never breaks His word. We look back on the enslaved Hebrews as well as the enslavement of our ancestors so that we may find the strength to move forward with hope as we keep God's promises foremost in our minds.

Our Christian hope is an attitude of assurance that God is current in the world and in the lives of His people to bring meaning, wholeness, and peace, even when the world is in despair. So, we must maintain our hope because it is the recognition and affirmation that when everything seems to be out of control, God remains in control. God is present in our lives, even in those places of darkness, oppression, and pain. God speaks over us as plainly as God did thousands of years ago: "Let my people go."

Creator God, help me to trust you for my deliverance. As I deal with the "pharaohs" in my life who seem to oppress me and make my life more burdensome, strengthen me to wait on your promises of liberation. In Jesus' name. Amen.

---

[1] "Moses, Hebrew Prophet," by Dewey M. Beegle, *Encyclopedia Britannica*.
[2] "Moses, Hebrew Prophet."
[3] *Nelson's New Illustrated Bible Manners and Customs How the People of the Bible Really Lived*, by Howard F. Vos (Thomas Nelson, 1999); Kindle edition.
[4] "Ramses II," by Peter F. Dorman, *Encyclopedia Britannica*.
[5] *The Five Books of Moses*, by Robert Alter (W. W. Norton, 2004); page 341.

5

Lesson 5
The Plagues
Exodus 7–10

A Hardened Heart

Today's Scripture text walks us through God's plan and actions to set the Israelites free; but within these chapters, there are practical and theological struggles that cannot be ignored. On one side, there is Pharaoh, the egotistical ruler of Egypt who was thought to be a god. On the other side are the representatives of the one true God: Moses, God's choice as leader of the children of Israel, and Aaron, Moses' brother and spokesman. The first showdown between the two sides didn't go as Moses and the children of Israel had hoped, but it had gone exactly as God had planned.

Pharaoh's refusal to liberate the Hebrews provided an opportunity for God to "multiply [God's] signs and wonders" and show God's mighty power and superiority to the supposed god by unleashing a series of plagues on the Egyptians. In the meantime, Moses continued to deliver to Pharaoh one simple message: "Thus says the Lord, the God of Israel, 'Let my people go'" (Exodus 5:1).

It's no surprise that Pharaoh adamantly refused to free the enslaved Hebrews. If he had, it would have been at great cost to him and to his country. At this

Difficult Bible passages make it hard to know what God is saying to us. An internet search may pull up a litany of opinions and emotional responses but not the truth of God's word. As students of the Bible, we can't always read the words on the page and take them at face value. In doing so, we may misinterpret God's word and violate Scripture. We have an obligation to "rightly [explain] the word of truth" (2 Timothy 2:15). To do that, we must:

time, Egypt had a population of around 10 to 12 million people, and the children of Israel made up approximately 2.5 to 3 million of that number. If they were set free, Egypt stood to lose 25 percent of its population and almost its entire work force. The effects would be devastating. Egypt's entire economy would collapse, the most basic services would be interrupted, and Egypt would become a bankrupt nation unlikely to ever attain its former greatness again.

So, from a practical standpoint, it's understandable that Pharaoh would refuse to free the Hebrews. And when confronted by Moses and Aaron with a message from a God whom Pharaoh did not know or acknowledge, Pharaoh showed his stubbornness and said no.

Exodus 7 opens with God giving Moses a divine strategy: "The LORD said to Moses, 'See, I have made you like God to Pharaoh, and your brother Aaron shall be your prophet. You shall speak all that I command you, and your brother Aaron shall tell Pharaoh to let the Israelites go out of his land. But I will harden Pharaoh's heart, and I will multiply my signs and wonders in the land of Egypt'" (verses 1-3).

In verses 9-14, Moses and Aaron confront Pharaoh again. God warned Moses that this time Pharaoh would ask for a sign that Moses had been sent by God. When Pharaoh told Moses to "perform a wonder," Aaron threw down his rod, and it turned into a serpent. Then Pharaoh's magicians did the same thing "with their enchantments" (verse 11). But Aaron's rod swallowed up the magicians' rods. Pharaoh wasn't impressed by this sign from God and made no concessions to free the Hebrews. Once again, Moses' meeting with the ruler didn't result in deliverance. Instead, it brought about more problems.

Verse 13 repeats a troubling phrase we've read before: "Pharaoh's heart was hardened." This phrase may be difficult to understand and raises many questions. Was that just or fair? How could Pharaoh be held accountable for what happened if God hardened his heart? God created human beings with free will so we can make our own choices. If God hardened his heart, isn't that a violation of Pharaoh's free will? This phrase seems to be ethically and theologically problematic. Even more confusing, the Book of Exodus uses different phrases to convey that Pharaoh had a hardened heart:

- God hardened Pharaoh's heart (Exodus 4:21; 7:3; 10:1; 11:10; 14:4).
- Pharaoh hardened his own heart (Exodus 8:15, 32; 9:34).
- Pharaoh's heart was hardened, but the Bible doesn't specify who hardened it (Exodus 8:19).

The most challenging question around this phrase is, Did God change Pharaoh's heart or his inherent nature to set in motion certain series of events? To give a faithful response to this question, we must do our due diligence and search the Scriptures. Considering the information given to us by the writer of the Book of Exodus about Pharaoh before and during his encounter with Moses, then the answer to our question would be no. God did not change Pharaoh's heart to set the pre-Exodus events in motion.

After careful research, it's evident there is nothing in recorded history that proves Pharaoh was ever sympathetic to the Hebrews at any point prior to his interaction with Moses—in fact, just the opposite. The Hebrews had become so numerous that the pharaohs perceived them as a potential threat, a threat they had unsuccessfully attempted to diminish by enslaving the Hebrews, demanding that midwives kill all Hebrew male babies at birth, and commanding the Egyptians to kill Hebrew baby boys by throwing them into the Nile River.

God didn't have to change Pharaoh's heart because Pharaoh already possessed a hardened heart. Instead,

God used Pharaoh's selfish decisions and cruelty to bring about divine deliverance to the children of Israel while giving glory to the one true God.

A hardened heart is a result of sin, and all of us have experienced its affects in our own lives. We may not rule over and enslave millions of people, but we've stubbornly refused to obey God's will, forgive others, or show love to our brothers and sisters. Our hardened hearts have affected our judgment and the decisions we've made. Like Pharaoh, we find it difficult to admit when we're wrong and repent. And while God doesn't harden our hearts, God may use them to get our attention with the purpose of getting us to repent so God can forgive us and draw us closer.

1. When have you had a hardened heart?

2. How did that affect your life in Christ?

3. What caused you to repent and turn to God?

Reading God's Word With Understanding

- **Pray.** We should ask God to give us wisdom and understanding concerning God's word. Ask God to help us to put our biases, preconceived notions, and pride aside so that as we read the Bible, we can hear from God's.

- **Be aware of translation difficulties.** The Bible was written in Hebrew, Greek, and Aramaic, not English. So, there are instances when understanding a Scripture passage may be difficult due to translation from the original language to another. We don't have to be Bible scholars or be fluent in the languages of the Bible to get a proper understanding. But reading a good concordance or Bible commentary can often shed much needed light on difficult passages.

- **Read the Bible in its proper context.** Sometimes we may be guilty of prooftexting when we try to explain what the Bible is saying. In other words, we may cherry-pick certain verses or passages to make a point. However, the Bible is best read in context, which may mean reading and understanding entire chapters or books to shed light on the meaning of a difficult passage.

- **Dig deeper into the text.** It's important to understand more than what the Bible might be saying to us in the modern world. To gain a richer knowledge of what God is saying across time starts with knowing who the original audience would have been. Who was God talking to? When did the intended audience live? What was their prevailing cultural context? What events sparked God's message to them?

When we take these steps to properly understand God's word and feel the power and life that comes from our study of the Bible, we can ensure that our theology is sound and biblically grounded.

God's Actions to Save His People

Over the centuries, scholars have debated the historicity of the plagues in the Book of Exodus. Some scholars claim the plagues did not happen but were merely symbolic literary inventions. Other scholars have tried to find a natural explanation for the plagues. Whatever the case, God would send a clear message that would ultimately result in the deliverance of God's people.

In each of the ten plagues, God would prove to Moses and the children of Israel that God is a promise-keeping God who would be faithful to the promise to free them. And God would show Pharaoh and the Egyptians that God alone is God, and God has no rivals, thus proving God's supremacy.

Plagues 1-3: Blood, Frogs, and Gnats (Exodus 7:15–8:20)

There were about 80 major deities in Egypt, all clustered around the three great natural forces of

The Nile River

At about 4,132 miles, the Nile River (Arabic, *Baḥr Al-Nīl* or *Nahr Al-Nīl*) is the longest river in the world. The name *Nile* is derived from the Greek *Neilos* (Latin: *Nilus*), which probably originated from the Semitic root *nahal*, meaning, "a valley or a river valley" and hence, by an extension of the meaning, "a river." The ancient Egyptians called the river Ar or Aur (Coptic: *Iaro*), "Black," in reference to the color of the sediments carried by the river when it is in flood. Nile mud is black enough to have given the land itself its oldest name, *Kem* or *Kemi*, which also means, "black" and signifies darkness.[1]

Egyptian life: the Nile River, the land, and the sky. If we study the ten plagues that God sent upon Egypt, we will discover that each one attacks something of vast importance or held sacred by Pharaoh and his people.

After Moses and Aaron had showed Pharaoh a miraculous sign, God instructed Moses to meet the ruler at the Nile River the next morning. The Nile was the lifeblood of Egypt. The Egyptians used this water source for almost everything, and without it, their land would have become a desert. The Nile formed the irrigation system that enabled them to grow crops. It was their water supply and the source of their food because fish was a staple in their diet.

First Plague: God turned the waters of the Nile River into blood: "'By this you shall know that I am the Lord.' See, with the staff that is in my hand I will strike the water that is in the Nile, and it shall be turned to blood. The fish in the river shall die, the river itself shall stink, and the Egyptians shall be unable to drink water from the Nile. The LORD said to Moses, 'Say to Aaron, "Take your staff and stretch out your hand over the waters of Egypt—over its rivers, its canals, and its ponds, and all its pools of water—so that they may become blood; and there shall be blood throughout the whole land of Egypt, even in vessels of wood and in vessels of stone"'" (Exodus 7:19).

At least three Egyptian gods were associated with the Nile: Osiris, the god of the Nile, who was depicted with the river running through his bloodstream; Nu, the god of life in the river; and Hapi, the god of the flood. When the Nile was turned to blood, it would force the Egyptians to question their gods. Where is Osiris, Nu, and Hapi? Why won't they deliver us or intervene on our behalf? But Osiris, Nu, and Hapi were revealed to be powerless, and Pharaoh's heart remained hardened. After a week, God sent Moses back to Pharaoh. The ultimatum was that if Pharaoh didn't free the children of Israel, God would send another plague.

Second Plague: God sent a swarm of frogs. But the frogs would not be contained in a few ponds. Rather, the frogs would be everywhere, from the river to the palace. They would be in the Egyptians' houses, beds, ovens, and food (Exodus 8:3-4). This was an attack on the Egyptian goddess Heket (Hay-ket), who was connected to life and fertility, especially childbirth. Women who gave birth wore amulets, small objects carved in the shape of frogs. These objects were supposed to have magical powers and religious significance. Heket was often pictured with the head of a frog and sometimes the body of a frog.

However, God demonstrated control of the symbol of fertility and would make the Egyptians despise the frogs that swarmed their land. God had turned their god against them. Thus, Pharaoh begged Moses to ask God to stop the frogs' invasion. Pharaoh promised that as soon as the frogs were gone, he would let God's people go. But once he found some level of relief, Pharaoh hardened his heart again and broke his promise. It was the first time Pharaoh went back on his word, but it would not be the last.

Third Plague: God struck the land with gnats. The gnats didn't correspond to any specific deity. However, the Egyptian worldview valued ecological harmony,

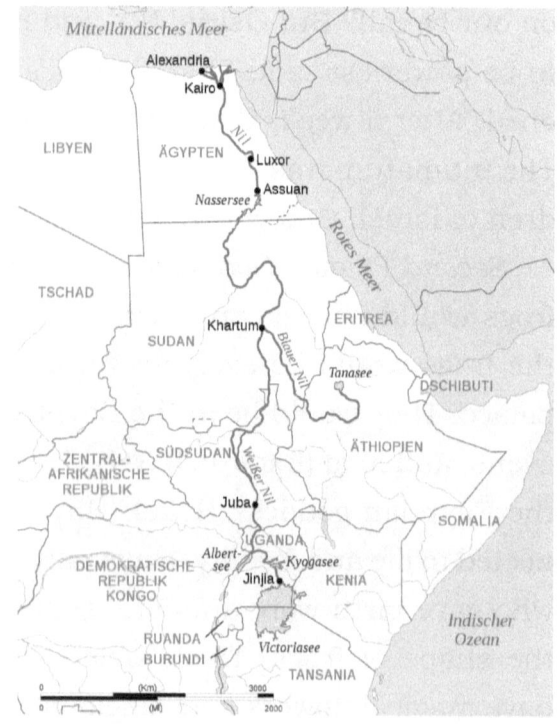

The Nile River, Egypt

and they viewed order from chaos as a vital part of the cosmic order. But God made it clear that God is the one who controls the natural elements. God can start and stop disasters at will.

There is another important distinction with this third plague. At the beginning of the first two plagues (blood, frogs) Pharaoh's magicians were able to replicate God's show of power with similar displays of magic with "their secret arts" (8:7). However, when the magicians tried to conjure gnats to try to match God's power, they were unable to do so, and "the magicians said to Pharaoh, 'This is the finger of God!' " (verse 19). But it did not make a difference in how Pharaoh perceived God and God's power. Pharaoh's heart remained hardened.

Plagues 4-6: Flies, Livestock, Boils (Exodus 8:20–9:12)

Fourth Plague: God sent an infestation of flies. But God also made it clear that from this point on, the plagues would harm only the Egyptians and not the Hebrews: "But on that day I will set apart the land of Goshen, where my people live, so that no swarms of flies shall be there, that you may know that I the LORD am in this land. Thus I will make a distinction between my people and your people" (Exodus 8:22-23).

There were flies everywhere, buzzing in the ears of every Egyptian. "In all of Egypt the land was ruined because of the flies" (verse 24). Pharaoh promised to allow the Hebrews to leave to worship God. But when the Lord lifted the infestation, Pharaoh once again reneged on his promise and would not let the Hebrew go.

Fifth Plague: The Egyptians' livestock died. This was a judgment against the goddess Hathor and the god Apis, who were depicted as cattle. Exodus 9:3 says that the Egyptians' horses, donkeys, camels, herds, and flocks died. The Hebrews' livestock weren't affected; thus they suffered no loss. Pharaoh asked specifically if the Hebrews had lost any livestock. When he found that they hadn't, his heart was hardened, and he refused to relent. The Lord told Moses to "take handfuls of soot from the kiln, and let Moses throw it in the air in the sight of Pharaoh" (verse 8). When the dust settled, it became the sixth plague.

Sixth Plague: God struck the Egyptians and their animals with boils. This was a plague against several gods who were associated with health and disease, such as Sekhmet, Sunu, and Isis. Even the magicians were struck with boils and couldn't appear before Pharaoh (verse 11).

Egypt was well-known for its medical advances. But when God demonstrated power by attacking the health of the Egyptians and their animals, there was no god who had the power to reverse the outbreak of boils and heal them.

Plagues 7-9: Hail and Lightening, Locusts, Darkness (Exodus 9:13–10:29)

Seventh Plague: Hail and lightning fell from the sky. Hail did not normally fall in Egypt. This plague was an attack on Nut, the sky goddess; Osiris, the crop fertility god; and Set, the storm god. The hailstorm accompanied by fire ran along the ground, and everything left out in the open was devastated by the hail and the fire. Once again, the Egyptian gods and goddesses were proven useless and helpless.

Moses delivered God's message to Pharaoh: "By now I could have stretched out my hand and struck you and your people with pestilence, and you would have been cut off from the earth. But this is why I have let you live: to show you my power, and to make my name resound through all the earth" (verse 15-16).

But this time, God gave the Egyptians an opportunity to avoid harm from this plague. Moses told them that to preserve their livestock, slaves, and anything of value, they had to remove everything from the open field. If they did so, their possessions would be saved. If they didn't, all they owned would be destroyed. Some of the Egyptian officials obeyed Moses, and their possessions were unscathed. But everyone else's possessions were destroyed. And the Israelites in Goshen were once again spared the destruction (9:19-26).

Eighth Plague: God sent a swarm of locusts. Although most crops were destroyed during the hail and lightning storm, there were latter crops of wheat and rye that appeared in the fields after the storm. But the insects affected those crops and devoured them, so there would be no harvest in Egypt that year. Where was Nepit, the goddess of the grain, or Min, the deity of the harvest? They proved to be useless against the Hebrews' God.

Ninth Plague: Egypt was plunged into deep darkness for three days. The Egyptians served Horus, the god of the sunrise; Aten, the god of the round, midday sun; and Atum, the god of the sunset. But the supreme deity in their national pantheon was Ra. This plague was aimed at the sun god, Ra, who was symbolized by Pharaoh. Pharaoh considered himself to be Ra incarnate. Thus, God saved the biggest deity for last.

Ra was not difficult to defeat. All God had to do was to shut out the light. The so-called great god of the sky, Ra, was blotted out. But the Israelites had light where they lived.

The darkness was so thick, the Egyptians couldn't see to walk from one place to another or see one another. They stumbled around their homes, paralyzed by the darkness. They must have been stunned by the failure of Ra and Pharaoh to save them. That seemed to prove that even the light of day was controlled by the all-powerful God of the Hebrews. With this plague, God demonstrated His power over all the gods and goddesses of Egypt, including Pharaoh.

But despite God's show of might and power, Pharaoh's heart was hardened again. And he told Moses, "Get away from me! Take care that you do not see my face again, for on the day you see my face you shall die" (10:28). He was right. He would never see Moses' face again. However, God wasn't finished with Pharaoh and Egypt just yet. God told Moses, "I will bring one more plague upon Pharaoh and upon Egypt; afterwards he will let you go from here; indeed, when he lets you go, he will drive you away." (Exodus 11:1).

When, like Pharaoh, all our fighting against God has been proved futile, and when our plans come to nothing, we can submit to God's will or rage in vain with a plagued heart. God is gracious and merciful, but sometimes we enter the danger zone when we ignore God's warnings and the truth of His word. When we do, we fall into sin and our hearts are hardened. The writer of the Book of Hebrews wrote, "Do not harden your hearts as in the rebellion, as on the day of testing in the wilderness, . . . As it is said, 'Today, if you hear his voice, do not harden your hearts as in the rebellion.' . . . again he sets a certain day—'today'—saying through David much later, in the words already quoted, 'Today, if you hear his voice, do not harden your hearts'" (Hebrews 3:8, 15; 4:7).

God was teaching Pharaoh that there is nothing more powerful than the power of God; and the aim of everything is to magnify, acknowledge, glorify, and worship God. Any attempt to magnify and worship something else, as Pharaoh and the Egyptians did, is in vain, for God is supreme over all rivals because there is no one like Him.

1. Reread the material on each of the nine plagues featured in this chapter. What similarities and distinctions did you discover?

2. Think about Pharaoh's continued stubbornness and hardness of heart. In the face of God's will for you, when have you experienced stubbornness and hardness of heart?

3. How does God use what's already in our hearts to get out attention and get the glory?

Reflect and Pray

We live in uncertain times, and it is easy to become discouraged. But as people of God, we shouldn't place our ultimate hope in the rulers of this age, in the pharaohs or the gods of this world, nor in the state of our economy. Our ultimate hope is in the sovereignty and the supremacy of God and Christ the Creator of the universe. The supremacy of God and of Jesus teaches us that God is not simply a spiritual being above the rest, but He is sovereign over all!

Almighty God, I acknowledge Your power over everything and everyone in Your creation. Forgive me for hardening my heart and for refusing to do Your will. Help me to repent and turn to You so that You may be glorified. In Jesus' name. Amen.

---

[1]From "Nile River," by Magdi M. El-Kammmash, and "Nile River Summary," *Encyclopedia Britannica*.

6

Lesson 6
Saved by the Blood
Exodus 11:1-5; 12:1-14, 21-28

God's Final Warning to Pharaoh

After many warnings, Pharaoh did not change his mind about releasing the enslaved Hebrews. God sent nine plagues upon Egypt, but once the plagues were lifted, Pharaoh broke his promises to free the Hebrews.

God then sent the tenth and final plague, the most horrific of them all. If Pharaoh didn't concede this time, all the firstborn of Egypt would die at the hands of the destroyer, the angel of death. Many of us are troubled by the account of so much needless violence and death, but in this lesson, we will explore how the most horrific of circumstances can lead to life and salvation.

Moses received instructions from God to prepare the children of Israel for their freedom, but there were several actions God wanted them to take before they left Egypt for the last time. These instructions included the first celebration of the Passover commemorating God's protection of the Hebrew households from the death angel. But they would only be protected if they obeyed God's instructions to the letter and positioned themselves for freedom.

Some warnings seem absurd or obvious, so we ignore them. However, not all warnings, regardless of how absurd or obvious they may seem, should not be ignored. God's warnings are of such import that they should never be ignored. For example, God sent Pharaoh messages, miracles, and warnings through Moses and Aaron to warn him what would happen if he didn't free the enslaved Hebrews.

The warnings took the form of plagues. In Lesson 5, we looked at the first nine plagues. As terrible as they were, they were mere annoyances and inconveniences compared to the tenth plague. Before each of the plagues, Moses delivered God's warning, but Pharaoh ignored Moses, Aaron, God's warnings, and his own officials.

After the plagues wreaked havoc on Pharaoh and his people, Pharaoh promised to let the Hebrews go and begged Moses to pray that God would stop His judgment on them. But after God lifted each plague, Pharaoh's heart was hardened, and he would once again refuse to let the Hebrews go. Because of his stubbornness, his people would continue to suffer; and during the final plague, they would pay dearly.

Tenth Plague: Death of the Firstborn (Exodus 12:29-30). "The LORD said to Moses, I will bring one more plague upon Pharaoh and upon Egypt; afterwards he will let you go from here; indeed, when he lets you go, he will drive you away. . . . Every firstborn in the land of Egypt shall die, from the firstborn of Pharaoh who sits on his throne to the firstborn of the female slave who is behind the handmill, and all the firstborn of the livestock. Then there will be a loud cry throughout the whole land of Egypt, such as has never been nor will ever be again" (Exodus 11:1, 5-6).

When reading about the plagues in these Scripture passages, people often focus mostly on the tenth plague and argue that the God of the Old Testament is a cruel and violent God. Where is the grace, love, and mercy of the New Testament God? This approach to the study of pre-Exodus events is devoid of context, but remember that the tenth plague was the last plague, not the first. The death of the firstborn was preceded by messages and warnings and nine other plagues. At any time before the tenth plague, Pharaoh had ample opportunity to heed God's warnings and free the Hebrews.

If we've read all the way up to the tenth plague, we will have witnessed God's patience and longsuffering with Pharaoh. God was not under any obligation to continue to extend to Pharaoh multiple warnings and opportunities to obey God's will, but God gave the ruler every chance to change his mind.

We may not understand God's mercy in the face of Pharaoh's stubbornness and cruelty, but the psalmist talked of God's mercy: "The LORD is merciful and gracious, slow to anger and abounding in steadfast love" (Psalm 114:4). Paul wrote, "For he says to Moses, 'I will have mercy on whom I have mercy, and I will have compassion on whom I have compassion'" (Romans 9:15). And the apostle Peter wrote, "The Lord is not slow about his promise, as some think of slowness, but is patient with you, not wanting any

103

to perish, but all to come to repentance" (2 Peter 3:9). God has vast capacity to show mercy, but it's up to us to accept that mercy and repent.

Another thing to consider about the tenth plague is that killing babies wasn't unprecedented in Egypt. This is a troubling reality, but remember, a previous pharaoh ordered the destruction of newborn Hebrew males some 80 years before. So, the destruction of the firstborn did not originate with Moses or with God. In Exodus 4, Moses warned Pharaoh that the way previous rulers treated God's firstborn would determine how God treated Egypt's firstborn. This is an example of sin cannibalizing itself so that the sins of the fathers fall upon later generations. Compensation is a fundamental law of life, and God is not unjust in permitting this law to operate in the world to bring about justice.

There are other biblical examples of the law of compensation. Jacob lied to his father, Isaac; years later, Jacob's sons lied to him. David committed adultery and had the woman's husband murdered. He also had numerous wives. Years later, his son Solomon engaged in polygamy, and two of David's sons were murdered. Haman built gallows on which to hang Mordecai, but it was Haman who was hanged there instead. One of the pharaohs ordered Jewish babies to be drowned in the Nile River; years later, God drowned Pharaoh's army in the Red Sea.

Those who commit evil will face the consequences, whether in the present or in eternity. The Bible says,

Tenth Plague: Death of the Firstborn

"Do not be deceived, God is not mocked, for whatever a person's sows, that they will also reap" (Galatians 6:7).

God was fully aware of Egypt's cruelty to the Hebrews in the past. And although God gave Pharaoh opportunities to correct course and free the enslaved

Hebrews, Pharaoh had refused. So, the only way forward was to finally and ultimately break Pharaoh's pride. If we don't consider this tenth plague in its proper context, we may conclude that God was cruel and insensitive. If this is how we approach these passages, we will miss God's grace toward Pharaoh and the Egyptians, grace that eventually ran out and led to judgment because Pharaoh refused to accept that mercy.

But the question remains: Does one crime justify another? The Old Testament scholar Terrence Fretheim states that violence and wrath "are not divine attributes"; rather, they are a response to human sins of violence.[1] Thus, God uses violence for two reasons: salvation and judgment.[2] God deals with the penalties of existing sin: Sometimes God is active; other times passive. God's violence, other than the sacrifice of Isaac, is connected to human transgressions. God uses violence to deliver people from violence, for example, the Hebrews in Egypt, the Jews in Germany, enslaved Africans in the United States.

Divine violence depicted in the Bible is problematic at best, ambiguous at the least. While we do not excuse the divine violence of murder, abuse, genocide, God out of His loving purposes, decides to engage in violence so that evil will not triumph. Violence associated with God "is 'not blind or unbridled violence,' but purposeful in the service of a nonviolent end. In other words, God's violence, whether in judgment or salvation, is never an end in itself, but is always exercised in the service of God's more comprehensive salvific purposes for creation."³

1. Have you ever questioned God's use of violence in the Bible or in modern times?

2. How does putting God's use of violence in context help you understand the bigger purpose of judgment and salvation?

3. What connections does the tenth plague (death of the firstborn) have to the cruelty of previous pharaohs? (their edicts sent to midwives to kill all male Hebrew babies as they were born or ordering soldiers to kill all male Hebrew boys)

The Passover

Once we understand the context of God's use of violence and judgment in the tenth plague, then we can see the salvation that results from it. In Exodus 12, God gives Moses detailed instructions that will prepare the children of Israel for deliverance. It's a long list, but God expected them to follow everything He commanded. They were told what to eat and how it was to be eaten. God didn't choose the food because of its nutritional content or flavor. Instead, the food

Passover Seder Plate includes a shankbone (zeroah), a roasted hard-boiled egg (beitzah), horseradish (maror/chazeret), onion (karpas), charoset, and parsley (maror/chazeret).

God instructed the Hebrews to eat was symbolic and would help them remember the events of Egypt and the Passover for generations to come.

When the children of Israel ate the Passover meal, they were to do so with their belts on their waist, sandals on their feet, and staffs in hand, ready to leave when God told them to. This possibly meant that they were probably supposed to eat the meal standing up, ready to leave Egypt at a moment's notice.

The main course of this meal was lamb, which God told them to choose on the tenth day of the first month and slaughter on the fourteenth day. This instruction was given to Israel to create a brand-new calendar.

This new day would mark the beginning of months for them. In a clear way, God was marking time for the Israelites according to their truest reality, which was found in their new life with God.

We all mark time. We do it with apps that help us manage our work, with calendars that help us arrange our schedules, with certain holidays and civic events that shape the way we plan our life together, and with clocks and watches that help us keep track of minutes and hours. The people of God have marked time by the weekly celebration of Christ's resurrection, the seasons of the church year, and occasional feasts that invite us into a way of organizing our life according to the story of God. By arranging time, we recognize that our truest reality is not set by the calendars of the empires of this world, but by the narrative of the God who calls us to freedom from oppression and death.

When the Lord liberates us from the bondage and penalty of sin, it's the dawning of a new day and the beginning of a new life. Everything old has passed away . . . everything has become new (2 Corinthians 5:17). The Passover meal marked the beginning of the religious year, but the real focus for the children of Israel was on the lamb and its blood. God's instructions called for a year-old male lamb, without blemish or defect, to be slaughtered. The meat was not to be eaten raw or boiled, but it had to be roasted by fire.

As for the lamb's blood, God instructed the people to take the blood and put it on the doorposts and the lintels of their houses where they would be eating.

When the destroyer, the death angel, arrived to slay the firstborn and the livestock in Egypt, he would see the blood, pass over their houses, and not strike them. The death angel would be looking for the lamb's blood on the outside of the house; he wouldn't be looking for the Hebrews' good works, efforts, talents, or possessions.

This event in the Hebrews' history is called Passover because it celebrates the death angel passing over the people's houses where there was blood and not destroying them. The command to place the lambs' blood on the doorpost and lintel probably sounded strange to the children of Israel. But when night came and the death angel passed over their houses without destroying them, they were glad they had obeyed God's instructions.

What God tells us to do does not always make sense to us; but when we obey God's instructions, the outcome makes it worth our initial confusion. God's thoughts and ways are as far apart from our thoughts and ways as heaven is from earth (Isaiah 55:8-9). When we can't see or understand what God is doing, we must remember that we are called to walk by faith, not by sight, and we can trust God and God's ultimate plans.

God's primary activity in the tenth plague was not killing the firstborn of Egypt, but in protecting people from the death angel who had come to destroy. In this way, the passing over was not so much the action of God skipping certain houses, but in covering those houses with a hand of protection so the destroyer could not enter and kill the firstborn. Exodus 12:23 indicates that there were two beings involved in the death of the firstborn: God, who protected certain houses, and the destroyer, who sought to destroy all but was kept from doing so in the blood-marked houses.

In verse 26, God told Moses, "When your children ask you, 'What do you mean by this observance?' you shall say, 'It is the passover sacrifice to the Lord, for he passed over the houses of the Israelites in Egypt, when he struck down the Egyptians but spared our houses.'" Then they bowed their heads and worshiped. This was the beginning of the Hebrews deliverance from Egyptian bondage.

1. How does the Passover show God's protection of the Hebrews?

2. What "Passover" event have you had in your life?

3. When has God delivered you and given you a fresh start and a new day?

The Passover meal, or *Seder*, is the traditional meal eaten during the Passover celebration. The word *Seder* means, "order," and is part of a longer ritual that includes different traditions referencing the pre-Exodus Passover the children of Israel participated in. This special meal is eaten on the first evening of Passover.

The ceremonial foods for the *Seder* help the participants tell the story of the Exodus. They are symbolic of certain aspects of the Passover that present-day Jews are to remember. These foods are arranged on a special plate called a *ka'arah*, or a *Seder* plate. The foods and their significance are:

- **Roasted Egg** (*beitzah*): A symbol of the festival sacrifice made in biblical times. The egg also symbolizes spring, the season when Passover occurs.
- **Shank Bone** (*zeroah*): Symbolic of the paschal lamb offered as the Passover sacrifice.
- **Bitter Herbs** (*maror*): Many people use horseradish as the bitter herb. This stands for the bitterness of Egyptian slavery. It's often dipped into the *charoset* to reduce its sharpness. *Maror* is eaten in accordance with Numbers 9:11 to eat the paschal lamb with unleavened bread and bitter herbs.
- **A Paste of Apple, Nuts, Spices, and Wine** (*charoset*): This symbolizes the mortar used by the Hebrews to construct Egyptian buildings.
- **Lettuce** (*chazeret*): This is considered another bitter herb along with the *maror*.

- **Parsley** (*karpas*): This is dipped in salt water and eaten. The salt water symbolizes the tears of the Hebrews during their Egyptian slavery.

The plate of ceremonial food is also presented with three pieces of *matzat* (unleavened bread) and a cup of wine. Two pieces of the *matzat* symbolize the double portion of manna the children of Israel gathered in the wilderness, and the third is used for breaking during the *Seder* to symbolize the brokenness of slavery. The wine is poured for the prophet Elijah. Traditionally, it's thought that the prophet visits each *Seder* meal, and it's hoped that he will bring about the messianic age (a time of peace and freedom for all).

The *Seder* meal is eaten as part of a longer ceremony that commemorates the stories around the Exodus. Traditionally, there are about 15 steps to the evening's celebration, including storytelling, drinking wine, singing, reading from the *Haggadah*, special blessings, and prayers.[4]

Behold the Lamb

After the children of Israel were delivered from slavery in Egypt, the Feast of Passover became a celebration of remembrance from that time forward. But the greatest celebration of the Passover occurred when Jesus celebrated with his disciples right before his crucifixion. At that fateful meal, Jesus revealed his role as the Paschal Lamb. However, his shed blood wouldn't save just one group of people. Rather, Jesus would die and shed his blood for the salvation of everyone.

From our communion services, we are familiar with Jesus' words as he celebrated Passover with the disciples: "While they were eating, Jesus took a loaf of bread, and after blessing it he broke it, gave it to the disciples, and said, 'Take, eat; this is my body.' Then he took a cup, and after giving thanks he gave it to them, saying, 'Drink from it, all of you; for this is my blood of the covenant, which is poured out for many for the forgiveness of sins. I tell you, I will never again drink of this fruit of the vine until that day when I drink it new with you in my Father's kingdom.'"

For Christians, the Passover points to a greater reality. We, like the children of Israel, needed the blood of a lamb without blemish. But this blood wouldn't cover the doorposts and lintels of our houses; rather, it would wash away our sin. Since God could not find anyone to lean on, God leaned on God's self and wrapped God's self in human flesh to create the perfect sacrificial Lamb in the person of Jesus Christ.

Jesus was such a perfect sacrifice that John the Baptist proclaimed, "Behold! The Lamb of God who takes away the sin of the world!" Another John, John the Revelator, said he heard in a vision the voice of many angels around the throne, the living creatures, and the elders; and the number of them was ten thousand, times ten thousand, and thousands of thousands, saying with a loud voice, "Worthy is the

Lamb who was slain, to receive power, and riches, and wisdom, and strength, and honor, and glory, and blessing!"

1. Why was Jesus the perfect sacrificial Lamb?

2. What is the significance of Jesus' shed blood in our salvation?

3. Read the Scripture passages where John the Baptist and John the Revelator make declarations about the Lamb. What can you declare about Jesus Christ, the Lamb?

Reflect and Pray

The plagues came to a tragic end for Pharaoh and the Egyptians with the death of the firstborn. This tenth plague is a troubling event that raises many questions for believers and nonbelievers alike. But when we study these and other difficult Scriptures in their proper context, it becomes clear that God is not capricious, cruel, violent, and uncaring. Instead, God works through our sin and capacity for evil and cruelty to achieve God's will in the world.

If only Pharaoh had obeyed God's warnings from the beginning. How different that outcome would have been. This is a wakeup call for us. When God speaks to us, we should listen and obey. The more we ignore God's voice, the tougher the consequences will be for us to face.

But after over 400 years of being enslaved in Egypt, the Hebrews were finally poised for deliverance. They were on the precipice of freedom. But before they could leave the land of their bondage, God had final instructions for them. They had to celebrate the Passover with a special meal and the blood of an unblemished lamb. By being obedient to God's instructions, they avoided being visited by the death angel, and their firstborn were spared.

There is protection and salvation in the blood of the lamb, but for Christians today, this Lamb is the Paschal Lamb, the ultimate and perfect sacrifice: Jesus Christ. Through the person of Jesus Christ, we are saved by the blood!

Lord, I may not always understand how You work through the evil and cruelty in this world to bring about Your will, but help me to trust You and have

faith in You. Thank you for Your perfect sacrifice on the cross, for the shedding of Your blood, and for the salvation You've so freely given. In Jesus' name. Amen.

---

[1] "God and Violence in the Old Testament," by Terence Fretheim, *Word & World*, Volume 24, Number 1 (Luther Seminary, 2004); page 22.
[2] "God and Violence in the Old Testament," pages 22-23.
[3] "God and Violence in the Old Testament," page 8.
[4] "What to Expect at a Passover Seder," by Rabbi Debbi Stiel, and "Learn About the Passover Seder Plate," ReformJudaism.org.

7

Lesson 7
Not So Fast
Exodus 13:17-22; 14:10-14

Are We There Yet?

Moses had prepared the people for freedom. Finally, after over 400 years of slavery in Egypt, the children of Israel would no longer call that country home. But what now? God had promised the people "a good and broad land, a land flowing with milk and honey" (Exodus 3:8), so that was their destination. How would they get there? The answer to that question was a bit more complicated.

If we map out the distance between Egypt and Canaan, the Hebrews' Promised Land, we will discover that the trip should have taken the people approximately only eleven days if they took the quickest route. But God didn't instruct Moses to travel that way. Instead, God chose a route that would keep the children of Israel in the wilderness between Egypt and Canaan for 40 years!

Exodus 13:17-18 says, "When Pharaoh let the people go, God did not lead them by way of the land of the Philistines, although that was nearer; for God thought, 'If the people face war, they may change their minds and return to Egypt.' So, God led the people by *the roundabout way* of the wilderness towards the Red

Sea. The Israelites went up out of the land of Egypt prepared for battle" (emphasis added). A journey that should have taken less than two weeks to complete would take four decades. After over 400 years in slavery, didn't the children of Israel deserve an end to their suffering? Why would God seem to prolong their wait for complete deliverance?

The Hebrews' predicament was not an accident. Their circuitous route in the wilderness wasn't because Moses made a wrong turn, neither did he miscalculate the length of their journey. The children of Israel were where they were because God led them there knowing exactly how long it would take. God knew that the shortest way was not the best way because the shorter, more direct route would take the children of Israel through enemy territory.

Northern Sinai was a militarized zone. The Egyptian army maintained a strong military presence in the region. There were also Philistines in the area. So, even if the Israelites somehow managed to fight their way through Sinai, they would still have to fight off the Philistines. God knew that the Israelites, though armed for battle, were in no condition to fight. God knew that once they encountered opposition, they would go back to Egypt believing that their life there was easier.

Understanding this divine concern for Israel is important because it shows that God's plans for Israel, and for us, considers every aspect of life. God considers prevailing spiritual maturity, emotional and mental health, physical abilities, financial readiness, and sociopolitical forces when charting a way into the future. When we read this passage, perhaps we think that God should have removed the enemy. However, the exercise of divine power in providential activity does not always ignore or override whatever obstacles might be in our way, particularly when the presence of those obstacles will make us better, stronger, or wiser.

Why doesn't God lead us directly to our blessings? Maybe we're not always ready when we think we are.

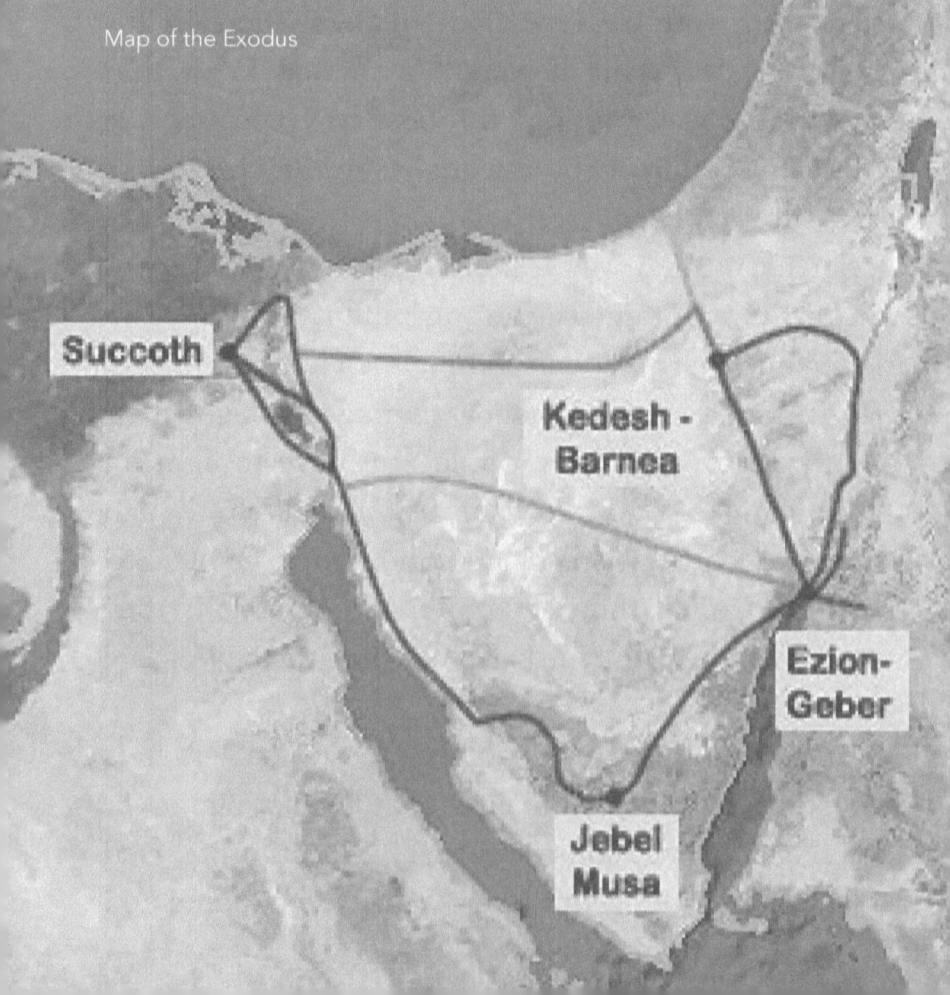

Map of the Exodus

Perhaps the longer journey will help us to move closer to who God wants us to be. We may not initially have the emotional, psychological, or spiritual strength for the direct route because we need more time and experience to mature and develop.

God is under no obligation to speed up the processes because of our impatience. So, instead of complaining about the journey or asking God, "Are we there yet?" perhaps we should learn to enjoy where we are until God leads us to our destination. Wherever we are, we can be assured of God's presence.

Verses 21-22 say, "The LORD went in front of them in a pillar of cloud by day, to lead them along the way, and in a pillar of fire by night, to give them light, so that they might travel by day and by night. Neither the pillar of cloud by day nor the pillar of fire by night left its place in front of the people." Why would God show up as a pillar of cloud and a pillar of fire? Throughout Scripture, clouds and fire are associated with the presence of God. They were visible symbols of an invisible God.

According to verse 22, "Neither the pillar of cloud by day nor the pillar of fire by night left its place in front of the people." Wherever the pillar of cloud by day and the pillar of fire moved, that's where Moses and the children of Israel moved. Day or night, if Moses and the children of Israel wanted to know where God was, all they had to do was look up, and they could see God's unquestionable presence.

1. When have you grown impatient on your walk with the Lord?

2. Are there times you can look back on and see that the longer route was the best route? If so, why?

3. What are ways you can learn to enjoy where God has you right now?

Stand Still

Finally, Moses was leading Israel, the chosen people of God, to their promised freedom. However, Pharaoh was up to his old tricks. During each of the plagues, Pharaoh called for Moses and promised him that if Moses would pray to God to lift the plague, Pharaoh would let the Hebrews go. After the tenth plague, the death of the firstborn, Pharaoh had finally freed the enslaved Hebrews. But as soon as they began their journey to freedom, Pharaoh changed his mind once again. He called together his troops to pursue and recapture Moses and the children of Israel and bring them back to captivity.

In the meantime, the Israelites were rejoicing as they struck out for Canaan; but soon their joy would turn to terror. In the rear of the ranks, they heard a thunderous sound, saw clouds of dust, and noticed Pharaoh's army rapidly approaching and closing in from the rear. Where would they go to escape? With the Egyptian army behind them, the impenetrable mountainous heights to the right and to the left, and the deep waters of the Red Sea before them, they were trapped. In fear and disbelief, the people turned on Moses.

"Was it because there were no graves in Egypt that you have taken us away to die in the wilderness? What have you done to us, bringing us out of Egypt? Is this not the very thing we told you in Egypt, 'Let us alone and let us serve the Egyptians'? For it would have been better for us to serve the Egyptians than to die in the wilderness" (verses 11-12).

The children of Israel accused Moses of ulterior motives. They believed he had brought them out into the wilderness to die. Feeling trapped and angry, they believed they had it better as slaves in Egypt. When emotions run high, it's easy to be shortsighted. How quickly they had forgotten the cruelty of their enslavement in Egypt, where they continually felt the taskmaster's whip on their back and live under Pharaoh's cruelty.

The Hebrews' desire to return to Egypt is typical of a people who have experienced an extensive period of oppression. Philosopher Paulo Freire writes, "The oppressed suffer from the duality which has established itself in their innermost being. They discover that without freedom they cannot exist authentically. Yet, although they desire authentic existence, they fear it. They are at one and the same time themselves and the oppressor whose consciousness they have internalized."¹

The oppressed must learn that the freedom they desire is acquired only by conquest, that a person must claim their own freedom because freedom is not something that can be given to a person by another. Novelist and activist James Baldwin said, "Freedom is not something that anybody can be given. Freedom is something people take, and people are as free as they want to be."²

The children of Israel were physically free from Egypt, but they were not mentally and emotionally free. As soon as they encountered trouble, they wanted to go back. Egypt specialized in graves. In fact, one third of Egypt's land was devoted to graves. The children of Israel believed they would have had a more decent burial in Egypt, which means they viewed their situation as hopeless. As the Red Sea raged before them, the children of Israel were, as the saying goes, between a rock and a hard place. When circumstances don't work out as we planned, there are times when we find ourselves there, too.

Being God's chosen leader, Moses understood why the children of Israel were so dispirited and angry. But he also knew that this wasn't the time for a lecture or a rebuke. Rather, Moses comforted them and spoke an oracle of salvation to a hurting and confused people, making clear the divine plan for them being at that precise place at that time. Moses wanted the people to see that they were right where God wanted them. Although the Egyptian army was bearing down on them, this wasn't a mistake; it was by divine design.

God never has an "oops" moment. God cannot err, and God cannot lie. God is always perfect, and God's plans for us are perfect. Sometimes even the difficult things in life are part of God's plan.

Moses encouraged the people in the face of anger and fear: "Do not be afraid, stand firm, and see the deliverance that the Lord will accomplish for you today; for the Egyptians whom you see today you shall never see again. The Lord will fight for you, and you have only to keep still" (verses 13-14). Imagine how these words might have been received by the Israelites.

They were on the banks of the Red Sea, with Pharaoh's army pressing in from behind. They had no boats to cross the sea, and they had no arsenal to equip them to fight off the Egyptians. They were no match for 600 Egyptian chariots driven by a skilled Egyptian charioteer and probably carrying a deadly Egyptian archer. They knew their situation was impossible, yet God's message to the children of Israel remained, "Do not be afraid."

God had a second word for the frightened Israelites: "Stand" (verse 13). In essence, God was saying to the Israelites, "I know the enemy is behind you, barriers or mountains are on each side of you, and you are staring at the Red Sea in front of you. But don't be afraid, don't turn and run, and don't surrender. Stand!" What does it mean to stand when we are facing a Red Sea situation?

The Red Sea

The Red Sea is a narrow body of water located between the Arabian Peninsula and Africa. It is about 1,200 miles long, has some of the hottest and saltiest seawater, and is difficult to navigate. Today, the Red Sea is one of the most traveled waterways in the world, transporting a heavy volume of traffic between Europe and Asia. Its name comes from the color change of the waters from blue green to reddish-brown due to the dying off the algae *Trichodesmium erythraeum*.[3]

To stand is to be in a physical posture of readiness. God told Israel to stand so they could have the right posture for when their deliverance came. If they ran away or bowed down, they wouldn't be ready for what God was about to do in their midst. Maybe the reason many of us are stuck at our Red Sea is because we are not in a posture of readiness. Even though the Lord is prepared to open doors of new opportunities, all we see are the problems in our life, which means we're not ready. But when we stand, we are in the right position of readiness for God to lead us through our Red Sea.

Israel was in a difficult place, but God spoke through their leader, Moses, to reassure them of His presence, to encourage them not to be afraid, but to stand. This wasn't what the people wanted to hear. It's human nature to want to do something—anything—when we encounter trouble. It seems counterintuitive to just stand around waiting for something to happen. Instead, our minds are whirring with exit strategies and things we can do to mitigate what's happening to us. But these are shortsighted plans, not God's. But when we stand still, we're able to see more of what God wants to reveal to us. How is it advantageous for you to stand still?

See the Salvation of the Lord

Not only did God tell the people to stand, but God wanted them to see what God was about to do: "Do not be afraid, stand firm, and see the deliverance that the LORD will accomplish for you today" (verse 13). Israel's problem, however, was they could see. They saw all too clearly that Pharaoh's army was approaching. What they couldn't see was how God would take their impossible predicament and use it for their deliverance and for God's glory.

Seventeenth-century English clergyman John Favel said, "Man's extremity is God's opportunity." It is one thing to believe that our extremity is God's opportunity when everything is calm, but it's another thing to realize the power of this truth during a raging storm. Our worst circumstance may be God's best opportunity to teach us always to trust God under all circumstances. In fact, our worst circumstances may be God's best opportunity to bring new meaning to our lives, to perfect us, or to fulfill God's purpose in our lives.

Whatever our personal troubles may be, God can use these moments to transcend our problems and deliver us. During what appeared to be a problematic situation, the children of Israel felt trapped and that all they had endured had been in vain. They thought their dream of freedom would be snuffed out before they had gotten to the Promised Land. But if they didn't stand still and see what God would do, they would miss God's miraculous deliverance.

We often miss what God is trying to do in our lives because we refuse to stand still long enough and look at what God is doing. Maybe we're in denial, and we won't accept what's happening to us. Or perhaps, like the children of Israel, we've accepted our fate, so we close our eyes and wait for the Egyptians to close in. But if we believe God to be the Almighty God who has all power, then we must open our eyes and see what God's doing in our midst. That's the only way we will be able to see God's deliverance.

As African Americans, we look back to our ancestors and see the injustices they lived with. We see the enslavement, the oppression, and the inequity enforced upon them. Was God blind to their suffering? Was God deaf to their cries for freedom and justice? Then we look around us today and see a violent world where many oppressed people still cry out for justice.

When life is difficult for us, we sometimes wonder if God sees us, if God knows and understands what we're facing. But there's a beautiful reminder tucked into the words of the prophet Hanani in 2 Chronicles 16:7-9: "For the eyes of the Lord range throughout the entire earth, to strengthen those whose heart is true to him." We serve a God who sees, who is all-knowing, and ever-present. Our God is continually aware of every detail of our lives, and God is looking to strengthen those of us who are willing to wholeheartedly place our trust in God.

The only thing the children of Israel could see was their geographical limitations. Unfortunately, they could not yet see God's salvation and deliverance as they stood on the banks of the Red Sea. Their sight was too one-dimensional to see what God was about to do.

During World War II, crews at Omaha Beach interviewed a soldier who had been at ground level. He saw soldiers all around him dying and said, "We're not going to make it." But another soldier in the same battle had an aerial view from a helicopter. That soldier said, "From what I see, we have the victory." From the ground perspective, the first soldier could only see what was around him. But with an aerial view, the solder in the helicopter could see the total picture.

God sees what we can't see on the ground. God also has an excellent aerial view, so that God sees the big picture. In fact, because God is the Creator God, God sees the end from the beginning. This all-seeing vantage point means that God knows more about what is happening and what will happen than we do. Therefore, we don't always understand God's plans or how they will be carried out. If we agree to follow God only when we understand what God is doing, we'll always stop short of experiencing God's inexplicable wonders, God's amazing grace, and God's wondrous power.

God did not bring Israel out of Egypt and to the Red Sea to shame them, destroy them, or to embarrass them. God's purpose for bringing them out was to let them see the salvation of the Lord. God was positioning them so that they would have a front-row seat to God's power over oppression, slavery, and bondage. Getting that far on their journey would have been a waste if God had planned for the Egyptians to simply ride out after them and retake them, hauling them back to Egypt and the slavery they had just escaped.

God's plans aren't haphazard and scattered. God's plans are well-coordinated, and they always serve a higher purpose. God coordinated everything so that the events of the Exodus would occur at the right time for Israel to see God's salvation and deliverance. The children of Israel may not have believed it then, but God had Israel walk at the right speed so that the Egyptians would not get to them before the appointed time. God then regulated the pressure of the Red Sea waters so that the winds from the four corners of the earth would blow the water into a heap and make a dry highway in the middle of the water just as the children of Israel needed to cross over. God found a place to pile up the water to keep it from creating a flood.

All of this was divine coordination and orchestration. God is the master strategist. God knows every move of the enemy before the battle begins. And just when our enemies think they have us hemmed in, God delivers us and gives us the victory. When God was finished working out a divine plan, not one Israelite life was lost, and not one Egyptian life was saved. This is the *totality of God's salvation and deliverance*. However, not only is there the totality of the Lord's deliverance, but there is also the *eternality of God's deliverance*. This means that God's deliverance lasts forever: "The Egyptian whom you see today you shall never see again" (verse 13).

The real reason God wanted Israel to see His salvation was so that they could become eyewitness of God's saving and delivering power. A witness must have personal and direct knowledge of an incident. If you talk about an incident that you have not seen with your own eyes, then you are not a witness. What you're saying is merely hearsay. But God wanted the people to have firsthand knowledge of God's capability to deliver, something they could bear witness to and share with generations to come.

1. What instances of salvation and deliverance have you seen in your life?

2. How does Moses' message to the children of Israel ("Stand still and see.") inspire you?

3. What may God want to show you today?

Reflect and Pray

After over 400 years of slavery in Egypt, the children of Israel were headed for the Promised Land. But why would it take them so long? And just when they thought they were home free, they found themselves in a terrible predicament. They thought they had seen the Egyptians for the last time as they were headed to freedom and the Promised Land. But one last time, Pharaoh broke his promise to let them go.

Now they were hemmed in by Pharaoh's army behind them, the mountains on either side, and the Red Sea stretched out before them. With seemingly no options, the people turned on Moses and accused him of wanting them to die in the wilderness. In their anger, they wished to be back in Egypt, the place of their enslavement.

But God had a plan the people didn't know about. God wanted to deliver the people in such a miraculous way that neither they nor Moses could take the credit for how they would escape. God was about to do something no one had ever seen, and God would ultimately get the glory.

As with the children of Israel, God wants us to stand still and see God's deliverance. God's way of saving us usually doesn't happen the way we think it should. But if we wait on God and trust God, we will be a witness to God's great and powerful work in our lives.

God, I know you're all-seeing and all-knowing. You see what I can't see. Sometimes I'm afraid when I feel trapped by my circumstances, and I can't see how You will deliver me. Help me to trust You, even amid chaos and trouble. Strengthen me to stand still and see Your salvation and deliverance so that I will be a witness to Your mighty power. In Jesus' name. Amen.

---

[1] *Pedagogy of the Oppressed*, Thirtieth Anniversary Edition, by Paulo Freire (The Continuum International Publishing Group, Inc., 2005); page 46.
[2] *Nobody Knows My Name*, by James Baldwin, Reissue Edition (Vintage, 1992); page 152.
[3] "Red Sea," by B. Charlotte Schreiber, and "Red Sea Summary," *Encyclopedia Britannica*.

8

Lesson 8
The God Who Fights Our Battles
Exodus 14:14-31; 15:1-21

The Battle Is the Lord's

In 1851, the British historian Edward S. Creasy published a book entitled *Fifteen Decisive Battles of the World.* It is, undoubtedly, the most famous work of military history of the nineteenth century. Creasy, however, chose only 15 battles out of a vast number of other critical battles, not for the number killed or wounded, the status or lore, nor their popularity. He selected the 15 battles listed in his book because he believed they changed the course of world history.

However, what could be more life-changing than to be in a battle you don't have to fight? Instead, you simply have to stand still and watch God fight the battle for you, a battle that will not only change the course of world history but will change our lives.

None of us can make light of the situation Moses and the children of Israel found themselves in. At some point in our lives, we—like Moses—had to learn how to handle difficult situations, our Red Sea experiences. But it raises the question, Why would God put the Israelites through this situation when they had already been through so much? One answer might be that God knew the Israelites would always live their lives in fear of Pharaoh's retaliation if they didn't confront him once and for all. They would never be fully able to trust God, and they would always be looking back over their shoulders, unless they knew beyond a shadow of a doubt that Pharaoh was no longer a threat to them.

God orchestrated these events so that the Egyptian army would be destroyed right before their eyes, so that the Israelites would know they did not need to live in fear. More important, God would fight for them if they obeyed God's instructions.

When God fights for us, God often uses unconventional weapons. The children of Israel were about to discover that God can turn instruments into weapons. God's can use anything not fit for battle and use it to win a battle. Who would ever think to use a cloud to fight a battle? God did! God placed a cloud between the Egyptians and the Israelites, with one side of the cloud giving off light, and the other side producing darkness. A careful study of the Scriptures will show us other times when God used unconventional weapons to win battles:

- God fought the battle for Gideon with a trumpet, an empty pitcher, and a lamp.
- God fought the battle for Joshua at Jericho with trumpets and a shout.
- God fought the battle for King Jehoshaphat and Judah with a few fearful people and praise singers.

- God fought the battle for Elijah on Mount Carmel with an altar.
- God fought the battle for David against Goliath with a slingshot and five smooth stones.

We don't have to be physically strong or possess a great artillery of weapons. We just have to stand still, hold our peace, place our situation in God's hands, and watch God use unconventional weapons and instruments to fight our battles.

Unfortunately, we sometimes think we are God's only option to win a battle. The prophet Elijah said, "I alone am left" (1 Kings 19:14). However, God informed Elijah that there were 7,000 others who had never bowed the knee to Baal (1 King 19:18). We are not God's only option. God can use unconventional weapons, unexpected people, and unusual instruments to accomplish His will.

The only time God will not fight for us is when we pick the fight. If we start the battle, God is not obligated to jump in and save us. Sometimes, we experience misfortune and don't get our desired outcome because we start fights we're not equipped to finish. That's not God's will for us. When he faced Goliath, David said, "For the battle is the Lord's and he will give you into our hand" (1 Samuel 1:47). If we want to be victorious, we must acknowledge that the battle belongs to the Lord, and it is for God to fight.

1. How do you feel knowing that the battle is the Lord's?

2. Have you ever been tempted to pick a fight? What happened?

3. What unconventional instruments has God used to fight battles for you?

Finally Free!

Finishing a story is one of the most important duties of a writer, but it is also one of the hardest. In writing a sermon, the most difficult part for me is not composing the body of the sermon, but writing the introduction and the climax. The climax is the moment when the rising action culminates and the story arc bends and begins its descent, known as "the falling action."

The word *climax* comes from a Greek word translated in English as "ladder." A good story will bring together all the tension that has been building since the exposition into one perfect scene that overwhelms the members of the audience and leaves them in awe. It is generally the high point at which the main characters face their biggest obstacle.

The Book of Exodus is such a great adventure that it has not one but three climactic moments. The first is when Israel crosses the Red Sea (Exodus 14). The second is when God gives the Law at Mount Sinai (Chapters 19–23). The third is when the glory of the Lord fills the Tabernacle (Chapter 40).

The first of these climactic moments may be the most famous event in the Hebrew Scriptures. This miraculous story has been acclaimed by composers, actors, novelists, and preachers. In the latter part of Exodus 14, God is about to set the captives free, but they will have to pass through what stands in their way.

Moses and the children of Israel were faced with a choice: Go backward or go forward. They had reached the climactic moment on their journey to the Promised Land, but the Red Sea stood in their way. They were faced with what appeared to be an impossible situation, but they were also getting ready to learn that impossible situations are no threat to a possible God. If we allow God to fight for us, God will always make a way for us, even if God has to split a sea to do it.

Moses delivered God's messages and instructions to the people. First, they were not to fear. Second, they were to stand still. Third, they would see the salvation of the Lord. Fourth, they would never see the Egyptians again because, fifth, God would fight for them. After these wonderful promises, God asked Moses, "Why do you cry out to me? Tell the Israelites to go forward" (verse 15).

The command to go forward did not make sense to the natural eye. But God will never ask us to do something without giving us what we need to do it. God had given Israel the unwavering assurance of His protection; all that was left was to go forward. But from where the children of Israel were standing, it looked impossible for them to go forward. They were facing a sea, and there wasn't a ship or a bridge to carry them across. But it was too late to go back.

Many of the Israelites said that they were going back and were not going to die in the wilderness. But when they turned and saw Pharaoh's troops behind them, pursuing them, they didn't have a choice but to go forward. Pharaoh's troops served their purpose. If they hadn't been bearing down on the children of Israel, perhaps many of them would have headed back to Egypt and all the oppression that they had left behind. Sometimes God places something behind us that makes it too costly for us to go backward.

God told Moses to lift his rod and stretch forth his hand over the sea and divide it. Then God ordered the clouds, the wind, and the angels to move on behalf of the people. God drove the sea back and turned the seabed into dry land so the children of Israel could cross over. This was a walk of faith. God didn't just open the sea and allow them to walk through it. That wouldn't be faith. Instead, with every step they took, God pushed the waters back and divided them.

They had to take that first uncertain step into the mud before they crossed over. It probably meant getting mud between their toes and on their clothes. Perhaps in the beginning it was messy. Taking that first step means walking into unknown territory. But God invites us to look ahead and imagine the new and bright future He has awaiting us.

How did the Israelites escape from Egypt? It was not just the wind and the tide. It was not poor strat-

Sarcophagus with relief of Israelites crossing the Red Sea in Split Archaeological Museum, Split, Croatia.

egy on the part of Pharaoh or an unexpected failure of military technology. It was not merely a sudden storm over the water. It was the power of God! If we have the faith, God has the power, and our faith with God's power can work miracles.

Pharaoh's army saw the newly dried ground and thought they could cross over behind the children of

Israel. But God told Moses to stretch out his hand over the sea again so that the waters would close upon the Egyptians. When Moses obeyed God, the water returned and consumed the enemy.

In the Jewish Chronicle, one of the authors discusses the parting of the Red Sea, which occurred seven days after the children of Israel left Egypt. This is why this story is read by the Jews annually on the seventh day of Pesach. The Talmud teaches that their personal elation should never make them forget the misfortunes afflicting others. So, during the *Seder*, or Passover meal, they spill drops of wine to remind them that their cup of deliverance and celebration cannot be full when others must suffer.

As we've mentioned in previous lessons, we must live with this dichotomy. If we are not happy that evil has been punished, then we do not care enough. But if we are not sad at the loss of life, then our humanity is weakened. "As I live, says the Lord God, I do not wish for the death of the wicked, but for the wicked to repent of their way, so that they may live" (Ezekiel 33:11).

The drowning of the Egyptian army raises important questions about the relationship between God's violence and human violence. Does liberation from tyranny require human or divine violence? While this text is a favorite of liberation theologians and those who have been oppressed, and who rightly value its theme of escape from bondage, its reception and use have been mixed. Some people have made God out to be cruel and insensitive because they are not reading this tragedy within its full context. Thus, we miss out on God's grace toward Pharaoh and the Egyptians, grace that eventually ran out and led to judgment.

God's patience for evil and unjust rulers does not continue forever. Actions such as oppressing the poor, torturing innocent people, and hatred and anger toward God and God's people do not go unnoticed. God's justice will be done. The punishment here, that the men of Pharaoh's army were drowned in the sea, echoes an earlier pharaoh's order that newborn Hebrew boys be drowned in the Nile River.

This echoes our discovery that God uses unconventional instruments to fight for the people of God. God doesn't use violence capriciously or because God cruel. Rather, God uses the violence and cruelty that already exists in our broken and sinful world as an instrument of judgment and salvation. While we don't rejoice in violence, even when used in our best interest, we can still worship and praise God for defending us and setting us free!

1. Have you ever waited a long time for deliverance? What happened?

2. What keeps you from going backward to your version of Egypt?

3. If you've been confused about how God uses violence in our world, after studying this lesson, how do you view it now? Have you changed your perspective? If so, why?

Song of the Redeemed

Singing can express joy or sorrow. We may sing when we're happy, or we may sing when we're depressed to lift our spirits. Enslaved Americans sang about their plight and their hope for a future free of shackles, chains, whips, toil, bondage, and injustice.

We tend to sing certain songs at particular seasons in our life because they conjure up certain images of past occasions and memories that encourage us in the present, or they paint a portrait of what we imagine the future to be. There is a profound connection between songs and memories. Like a scrapbook full of memories, God provided Israel with a song.

God placed an angel between Israel and the Egyptian army. Moses stretched out his hand over the sea, and the Lord swept back the sea by a strong east wind and turned the sea into dry land. The people, by faith, crossed on dry ground, and Pharaoh's chariots and army followed them. When the people reached the other side, God told Moses to stretch out his hand again. And when Moses stretched out his hand, the sea returned to normal, and Pharaoh's army drowned.

In the end, all the Egyptians who chased Israel were gone, drowned, or scattered on the side of the sea. This story has a dark, violent side. It is not for the faint of heart. Warfare never is. But what the Israelites saw in this warlike imagery was that, finally, someone had defended them and fought for them against enslavement, brutality, and death. We are grateful when God defeats our enemies. God's use of force against the power of oppression is not experienced as violent by those who are oppressed. We see God as the God of the oppressed, one who will fight our battles if we just keep still.

Finally free, the Israelites are now on the other side of the Red Sea safe from the Egyptians. Exodus 14:31 tells us that Israel saw the great work that the Lord did against the Egyptians. And in Exodus 15, they break into song and worship God. Their hearts were full, and their minds were free from worry. When God does something for us that we could have never accomplished on our own, the best thing we can give to let God know we are thankful is praise, and sometimes that praise can be in song.

Israel's deliverance was a moment of high experience. The hour was full of the sense of the greatness of life. The shackles were gone, the enemies were destroyed, freedom was theirs, and opportunities were before them. This sense of the greatness of life was created by the sense of the greatness of God. What could Moses and the children of Israel do other than sing and praise God?

Exodus 15 begins with a song celebrating a redemptive act of God. The history of salvation is sometimes described as a drama of redemption. Once we understand the essential role of music as a response to redemption, it becomes clear why Exodus 15 has to be a song. It is the first anthem recorded in the Bible, the first liturgy of liberation.

As the eminent preacher W. M. Taylor, remarked, "Long before the old ballads of Homer were sung through the streets of the Grecian cities, or the foundation of the seven-hilled metropolis of the ancient world of Rome was laid by the banks of the Tiber, this matchless ode . . . was chanted by the leader of the emancipated Hebrews on the Red Sea shore; and yet we have no polytheism, no foolish mythological story concerning gods and goddesses, no self-glorifying, but instead the firmest recognition of the personality, the supremacy, and holiness of an all-powerful God."[1]

When you read this song, you will notice that the first six verses are about God, while the rest of the song is addressed to God. Moses and the people sang *about* God, and then they sang *to* God, so everything about this song glorifies God. Moses made certain to ascribe every ounce of praise to the Lord Jehovah for redeeming Israel.

This song graphically portrays what God did to bring a people across the sea and glory to God. It gives such specific details that we can almost see the Exodus unfold before our eyes. Moses looked back on all that God had done to bring about deliverance. The whole point of remembering or looking back, as Moses did in this song, is to reflect on God's power in the past to increase our trust in God in the present.

If we look back, we will see that when things were at their worst, God was at God's best. Who God is and what God has done was written as a song so the people and future generations would know what God did for their ancestors.

Why not just write it as a letter or a story? Music tends to become embedded in our memory much quicker than the spoken word. How many times have we sung the ABC song to recall where a letter is in the alphabet? Perhaps we know of loved ones who remembered favorite hymns or songs as they were on their death bed. A snippet of a song can stir a deep memory. This narrative was put to song to glorify God and to help future generations never forget who God is and what God has done.

This song, however, was not simply Moses' song, which is why it is often referred to as the "Song of the Sea." The whole nation joined in the singing, forming a chorus of millions. The text also makes a special point of mentioning the involvement of the women. Exodus attributes the poem to Moses, with Miriam's rendition considered an antiphonal response. But several considerations support the possibility that, from a traditional historical perspective, the poem was Miriam's before it was Moses'. The words following the word "then" in verse 1 that begins this song is paraphrased by Miriam, who sings in verse 19, "When the horses of Pharaoh with his chariots and his chariot drivers went into the sea, the Lord brought back the waters of the sea upon them; but the Israelites walked through the sea on dry ground."

"Then the prophet Miriam, Aaron's sister, took a tambourine in her hand; and all the women went out after her with tambourines and with dancing. And Miriam sang to them: 'Sing to the LORD, for he has triumphed gloriously; horse and rider he has thrown into the sea.'" The song included a call and a response. The people sang, and Miriam and the other women played their tambourines and danced. (Although we met Miriam early in the Book of Exodus, this is the first time Miriam is mentioned by name.)

The song of salvation was for all God's people. It was not enough for Moses to sing it, or even for all the men of Israel to sing it. The women had seen the same salvation, and they were trusting in the same God, so they also praised God for victory at sea.

Miriam is to be recognized for not only being acknowledged as the first prophetess, but her dance began the Israelite tradition of celebrating God's victories through musical instruments and dance. Her liturgical tradition of dancing and singing Israel's victories would continue for generations to come.

Sacred dance and singing have been a facet of the worship practices of African Americans since these cultural expressions have been documented. Where the song represented the vocalization of praise, dance reflects the physical manifestation of praise. Early African American religious expression of song and dance demonstrated the relationship between music and movement within traditional African worship practices.

James Cone states, "There is no understanding of black worship apart from the rhythm of the song and sermon, the passion of prayer and testimony, the ecstasy of the shout and conversion as the people project their humanity in the togetherness of the Spirit. To shout is to 'get happy.'"[2] It is one's response to the movement of the Spirit. The authentic dimension of Black people's shouting is found in the joy the people experience when God's Spirit shows up in a mighty and powerful way as on the Day of Pentecost.

The only problem with Israel's actions is that they did not begin singing until their enemies drowned and their freedom was secured. Only then did they burst into a song of praise. Up to this moment, we have not heard a single note of praise. We don't read anywhere that while they were enslaved, in bondage, in captivity, or in front of the Red Sea that they sang.

This is a lesson to us. We shouldn't wait until we are delivered to sing, praise, and worship God. During our trials, we can sing, even if it's to lift our spirits. While we are facing what seems to be impossible situations, we should sing. Singing can promote an atmosphere of joy, lift our spirits, and remind us of how powerful and loving God is.

1. Do you wait until you're happy to sing? Why?

2. What does singing do for you?

3. What song can you sing to God now to express how you feel?

Reflect and Pray

In this lesson, we reached the first of three climactic moments in the Book of Exodus: the crossing of the Red Sea. But before the children of Israel could cross, they had to obey God's instructions, which included them standing still and watching God fight for them. God never asked them to gather up weapons and turn toward the Egyptians and fight. Instead, God fought for them.

Then God parted the Red Sea and told the people to go forward to freedom! But their deliverance wasn't final until God then closed the sea on the Egyptians and drowned them. Though we don't rejoice in the death of others, we can be elated that God delivered the Israelites as they made it safely to the other side, safe in the knowledge that the Egyptians would never bother them again.

And as a highlight of their victory celebration, we hear the people sing a song to and about the God who delivered them. It encourages us to sing not just when we've been set free, but even while we're still in the midst of our bondage. We can always sing and celebrate God's presence with us and thank God in advance for His deliverance!

Lord, thank you for fighting for me. There are times when I am tempted to fight my own battles because I don't always understand Your timing or Your plans. But enable me to wait on You, knowing You will be with me and make ways for me. In Jesus name. Amen.

---

[1] *Moses the Law-Giver*, by William Mackergo Taylor (Franklin Classics, 2018); pages 121-122.
[2] Practicing Our Faith: A Way of Life for a Searching People, edited by Dorothy C. Bass (Fortress Press, 2019); page 93.

9

Lesson 9

The Bitter Into Sweet

Exodus 15:22-27; 17:8-16

If It's Not One Thing, It's Another

In this lesson, we continue our journey with Moses and the children of Israel just as they enter the wilderness. It quickly becomes clear that they did not need tasks equal to their powers; they needed power equal to or greater than their tasks.

The Red Sea victory was an unforgettable event in the life of Moses and the children of Israel. The Egyptian army pursued them but were defeated. Moses and the children of Israel sang the great song of Moses and Miriam. We might think that their miraculous experience at the Red Sea would have put an end to their spiritual vacillation. However, the transition from the first part of Exodus 15—where they are singing, dancing, and rejoicing—took a sharp turn.

Scripture illustrates time after time that God's people are at their most vulnerable state following periods of victory. Andrew Bonar, a Scottish Presbyterian preacher of the nineteenth century, said, "Be as watchful after the victory as before the battle!" It is often after a great spiritual victory that the strength of our faith is tested.

Exodus 15:22 says, "Then Moses ordered Israel to set out from the Red Sea." The Hebrew verb tense used suggests that Moses had to apply effort to get the people of Israel to move on from the shores of the Red Sea. They had just experienced a great deliverance, and perhaps they were content to remain where they were. After all, they were out of Egypt, they were free, and their enemies were defeated, so why hurry? Maybe their celebration had led to what could have been complacency, a refusal to move forward to other challenges by which they could grow in their faith. One great victory, however, does not settle everything. We need challenging new experiences that will grow our faith and glorify God.

Once across the Red Sea, the Israelites went to Shur: "They went into the wilderness of Shur. They went for three days in the wilderness and found no water" (verse 22). The wilderness of Shur is an arid and sparsely populated wilderness region in the northern Sinai. Wilderness areas are difficult places to journey through. It is not an environment where drinking water is plentiful. It is not a place of ever-flowing streams, but of blistering heat, sandstorms, and sand dunes.

As Moses and the children of Israel entered the wilderness of Shur, they found no water for three days. With several million people and livestock in a hot climate and in a mostly hostile environment, water would be paramount. It did not take long to go from the problem of the Red Sea crisis to a water crisis. Water is essential for life, so this was an emergency. They would drink or die.

But just three days earlier, the people were singing the victory song of Moses and Miriam. Three days earlier, there was God-centered jubilation over the defeat of their enemy, and the people had high hopes for a brighter future. But as we come to verse 22, the music fades, the tambourines are silent, and soon Israel's antiphonal singing is replaced with antiphonal grumbling and complaining. Before they finished celebrating their victory over one trial, they faced another one.

As Christians, we know all too well how life can go from one trial or crisis to another. Life consists of ups and downs, highs and lows, valleys and mountains. Some days we find ourselves singing Moses and Miriam's song, and other days we hang our harps on the willows and sing Babylon's sad song.

At this point, everything seemed to be working against Moses and the children of Israel, so it is not hard to imagine their relief when they spotted a well in the distance. They hurried to this potentially life-giving water and scooped a handful of it into their mouths only to discover that the water was bitter. Its taste was unpleasant and salty. In disgust, the people yelled, "We can't drink this water!" They were extremely upset and named the place Marah, which means, "bitter." The water should have been lifesaving, sustaining, and satisfying, but it proved to be none of these things. Can you imagine Israel's disappointment at this unfulfilled expectation?

But Marah is not only a geographical location. Marah is a place on life's map. It's a place of circumstances, events, and experiences to which we often come to during our life's journey. Life can be bitter, and it may seem that we spend many seasons of life in Marah. Everyone, regardless of who we are, will come to bitter waters at some point in life: death of a loved one, sickness, bankruptcy, failed relationships, divorce, betrayal, false accusations, and rejection. It's not so important when we will eventually visit Marah, our place of bitterness; it's what we do while we're there that matters. Do we complain and become angry with God and other people? Or do we lean in and listen for what God may be trying to tell us there?

Israel arrived at Marah because God sent them there, which means they experienced their water crisis while they were on the path of obedience. They were not out of the will of God. Moses was leading them the way God wanted them to go. That means that obedience is no exemption from trial. Just because we are experiencing trials does not mean we are out of the will of God. Yes, we need to examine our hearts and lives to see whether troubles are chastisements for disobedience or sin. But while we are taking spiritual examination of ourselves, we should keep in mind that troubles and trials come to the godly while we're being obedient.

Everything, even the Marahs, the difficult things in life, can be part of God's plan. God orchestrates every move and event in our lives to serve a divinely designed purpose; and God always knows what God is doing, even when we find ourselves standing at the bitter waters of Marah.

"And the people complained against Moses, saying, 'What shall we drink?' " (verse 24). The people were tired and thirsty. They had just been disappointed by the bitter water, and tempers were running high. In verse 25, God puts the people to the test. Unfortunately, the people's experience there was just the beginning of how they would respond to future crises. Their continuous moaning, grumbling, and complaining would become a running theme throughout their wanderings.

By putting them to the test, did that mean God was delighted to see the people suffer? You have heard people say, "God tests us in order to find out what we're made of." But that's incorrect. The God who made us knows what we are made of. God knows whether we will pass the test. Tests are not for God's benefit; they are for our benefit. God was testing Israel, not because God did not know their hearts, but because they did not know their own hearts. God wanted to show them that instead of trusting the God of their salvation, they were complaining, murmuring, and grumbling.

One of the lessons we cannot miss in this story is how God's people responded to this test. Once again, the people took out their anger and frustration on Moses, their leader. However, Moses was not the reason for their problem. Instead, he would be the key to finding a remedy.

Many pastors can relate to Moses' dilemma. I have been in the pastorate for almost 30 years, so I know how church people think. As pastors, we may go to great lengths to help church members or those who come to church looking for support. We counsel with them, pray with them, and do our best to shepherd them through their difficulties. But if things don't work out the way they want them to, or if we say something they don't want to hear, they might take out their anger on us. Human beings can be fickle creatures. One day, we're proudly lauding our leaders; but the next day, we're vilifying and attacking them. That's why pastors have to always look to the Lord. We can't rely on the congregation to always be in our corner.

Moses responded to the people's complaints by interceding on their behalf through prayer to the Lord. Moses could have allowed their anger to discourage him. He could have turned away from God; instead, he turned to God. When Moses cried out to God, his one prayer accomplished more than all the complaining the Israelites were doing. God answered Moses by showing him a piece of wood, apparently a particular tree.

The word translated "showed" in verse 25 means, "to direct or instruct." God told Moses to throw the wood into the bitter water. Moses could have said to God, "These people are already questioning my leadership. Don't you think I've had enough humiliation for one day?" But Moses did what God commanded him to do. He threw the wood into the water, and the water instantly became sweet!

We may wonder if this was a genuine miracle, or whether the wood had some kind of natural healing effect. Scholars have tried to determine whether any of the trees in the Sinai Peninsula has the inherent ability to purify water. Perhaps there was a local remedy, some desert bush with the right chemical properties. However, no healing tree has been discovered. The text does not tell us what kind of tree it was nor what it was about the makeup of the tree that caused the bitter waters to become sweet.

The Jewish Midrash is a form of rabbinic literature that offers commentary or interpretation on biblical texts, specifically the first five books of the Hebrew Scriptures. It is suggesting that the wood Moses used may have been an olive tree, a willow tree, or a thistle bush. The consensus in these writings is that whatever kind of tree it was, its wood was bitter. We are bound to conclude that what happened at Marah was genuinely a supernatural miracle, something that only God could do.

God used bitter wood mixed with the bitter water to make the water sweet. In our understanding, bitter mixed with bitter equals bitter. But with God, bitter wood mixed with bitter water resulted in sweet water. If we set our hearts to be obedient to God's commands, no matter how strange and unusual they may sound, God can turn the bitter waters in our lives into something sweet.

This is not to suggest that life will suddenly become carefree and that we will move from one victory to the next if we are obedient. Rather, if we will accept by faith that God is with us wherever we go, that God is guiding our steps, that God is in control of our circumstances, God will provide what we need in God's perfect time.

God told Moses and Israel, "If you will listen carefully to the voice of the LORD your God, and do what is right in his sight, and give heed to his commandments and keep all his statutes, I will not bring upon you any of the diseases that I brought upon the Egyptians; for I am the LORD who heals you" (verse 26).

Here, God revealed another of God's divine names. The Israelites already knew God as the Great I AM, the eternal and self-existent God. They had also witnessed God as the God who hears, the God who rescues, and the God who provides. Now God is revealed as *Jehovah Rapha*, "the God who heals." *Rophe* refers to "wellness and soundness," physically and spiritually. It means, "to restore, to heal, to cure, not only in the physical sense but in the moral and spiritual sense also." At Marah, God demonstrated his healing power by curing the bitter waters.

The good news for the children of Israel, and for us, is that Marah is merely a camping ground. It is not a place to live. Marah is a thoroughfare, not our destination. God brings us to Marah, but He will not leave us there. So, we must not allow the devil to convince us that our bitter season will last forever. Not only can God make that which is bitter sweet and heal it, but we can be assured that just beyond Marah is a place of refreshing and blessings unlike anything we have ever experienced.

"Then they came to Elim, where there were twelve springs of water and seventy palm trees; and they camped there by the water" (Exodus 15:27). Elim is an oasis in the desert, a place of abundance, a place of refreshment. However, to get to Elim, you have to go through Marah. God wants to bring balance to our lives, so God gives us seasons in Marah, but God will also lead us to seasons in Elim.

It's interesting that there were only six miles between Marah and Elim. We know that now, but the children of Israel didn't know that as they sat in Marah complaining about the bitter water. What if they had known that they were only six miles from a place of abundance? The people of God were close to blessing and refreshment, but they had no idea how close they were. So near in life is sweetness to bitterness in every trial. Instead of murmuring at Marah, had they pushed on a little further, they would have arrived at Elim in about two hours. There, they would have found all they sought and more than they expected. Just a few steps can take us through the valley of the shadow of death out into the green pastures and beside the still waters.

1. When you've gone from victory to crisis or from one crisis to another, what did you do?

2. What is your Marah?

3. When has God turned the bitter into sweet for you?

How to Handle a Crisis

Believers are at their best when they encounter the storms of life and when the storm is over, they are still standing. Someone once said that people are not best known by how they act when things are in control, but how they react when things are beyond their control. In his book *Song of Glory*, William J. Reynolds tells the story of a man named Horatio G. Spafford, who was no stranger to trouble. Spafford came to a point in his life when he felt he could not go on. However, from that dark period in his life emerged his most memorable work.

Spafford was a prominent lawyer and senior partner in a large, thriving law firm. In October 1871, he invested much of his wealth in real estate but lost his extensive holdings in the Great Chicago Fire. On February 11, 1880, his son and namesake, Horatio Jr., died of scarlet fever at the age of three. His friends at the Presbyterian church he and his family attended misunderstood his son's illness. Thinking that the Spaffords were being punished for their sins, the church members asked the family to leave the church.

Spafford's greatest tragedy, however, occurred in 1873, when he and his family planned a trip to Europe, but last-minute business matters required him to remain in Chicago. Intending to join his family a few days later, he kissed his wife, Anna, and their four daughters, ages 2-11, and waved good-bye. The ship his family was on was struck in the middle of the Atlantic Ocean by a British iron sail ship, and in

12 minutes, the ship sunk. Anna survived, but their daughters drowned.

When Horatio Spafford received the tragic news, he sailed to join his wife in England, went to the area where his daughters died, entered his cabin, and wrote these familiar words: "When peace like a river, attendeth my way. When sorrows like sea billows roll. Whatever my lot, thou hast taught me to say, it is well, it is well, with my soul."

After God made the water at Marah palatable, Moses and the children of Israel traveled to the wilderness of Sin and encountered another crisis. They now had nothing to eat. The people murmured, and Moses did what every leader should do when they are faced with crisis: He prayed. After Moses prayed, God sent bread (manna) as well as quail from heaven every day, and God sent twice as much on the sixth day so the people would not have to cook on the seventh day, the sabbath.

The people had food to eat, but once again, they were without water. Moses prayed again. This time, God told Moses to strike a rock, and water would come out of it for the people to drink. Problem solved.

Not so fast. Verse 8 begins, "Then Amalek came." Amalek came and fought with Israel at Rephidim. Again, Israel experienced their greatest test after a great blessing. The apostle Paul warns us in 1 Corinthians 10:12: "If you think you are standing, watch out that you do not fall." Just because we have grown spiritually, can quote the Bible, don ecclesiastical garb, speak in unknown tongues, and have hands laid on us does not mean we have arrived. We must never forget that our greatest blessing may be a prelude to our greatest test.

This would be Israel's first military skirmish after leaving Egypt. Before this, they had not taken up arms against their oppressors or enemies. This was because they had someone to fight for them. The God of Israel won the battle for them. But now God was getting ready to send Moses and the children of Israel into their first battle as their survival was at stake at Rephidim. This time, they would have to stand and fight. They would be fighting in self-defense and waging a holy war fighting for the glory of God. This would be the first of many battles that God's people would fight before completing their conquest of Canaan.

For ancient Jewish readers, Amalek is swept into the long story of God's faithfulness to Israel, the complicated choosing of a king, and the protection of God's people from their enemies. It is one response to terror among the internal tensions of stories, prophecies, and teachings of compassion and forgiveness that directly contradict more violent commands. Those who faithfully and honestly bring a sound biblical and theological interpretation of Scripture show us how to live within the broad reach of the Bible.

Many of us read the Bible without having any experience of the kinds of enemies that ancient communities knew. The people born of Amalek wandered throughout the Hebrew Scriptures. They were a people who generations of interpreters have charged with moral depravity. The Amalekites hold an exceptional place in the Hebrew Scriptures. Unfortunately, no other people are assigned a permanent place of dishonor generation after generation like the Amalekites. Their story takes us deep into the landscape of Israel's generational trauma by being Israel's persistent enemy.

Amalek was the thirteenth son of Esau, one of the twin sons of Isaac. If the Amalekites are the descendants of Esau and the Israelites are the descendants of Jacob, Esau's brother, this means that the nation of the Amalekites were related to the Israelites. But because of the enmity between Jacob and Esau (Genesis 27), there was strife between the Amalekites and the Israelites. However, after 20 years, Jacob and Esau came back together (Genesis 33). Afterward, they went their separate ways, Jacob thinking everything was all right between them. But Esau still had a problem with Jacob.

So great was Esau's problem with Jacob that his great-grandson Amalek picked it up and passed it on to his children. The Amalekites hated Israel because of this family grudge, passed down from generation to generation. Throughout Israel's history, the Amalekites raised their heads. They were there in Saul's day. One of the most difficult passages is in 1 Samuel 15. God told Saul to attack the Amalekites and destroy all that they had. God told Saul not to spare them, to kill men, women, children, and livestock. Saul carried out the command, though he preserved everything of economic value, along with the Amalekite king Agag. Saul disobeyed God by sparing Agag.

David was a man of war, and he slaughtered the Amalekites, but a few got away. Years later, right before the restoration of the Jews, a woman by the name of Esther came along. She married King Ahasuerus, also known as King Xerxes. Esther had a first cousin named Mordecai, who was the son of Jair, the grandson of Shimei and the great-grandson of Kish the Benjamite, which means Mordecai was an Israelite.

Mordechai was disliked by Haman, who set up gallows to have Mordecai and the Jews slaughtered. Esther 3:1 tells us Haman was the son of Hammedatha the Agagite. An Agagite was a descendant of Agag, and Agag was the Amalekite king that Saul allowed to get away. So, Haman was an Amalekite, which means this grudge between the Amalekites and the Israelites continued from generation to generation just as Exodus 17:16 states. The Amalekites never forgot what happened to their great-grandfather Esau when his brother, Jacob, stole his birthright, and they were not going to let this happen again. They were going to keep their birthright.

Traditionally, Christians believe that the Hebrew Scriptures illustrate New Testament truths. Some would argue that in the Hebrew Scriptures, the Amalekites refer to what the New Testament calls "the flesh," and the Israelites refer to what the New Testament calls "the Spirit." So, the flesh (Amalekites) is on one side pulling us this way, and the Spirit (Israelites) is on the other side pulling us the opposite way. There is a war between the flesh and the Spirit. Which one do we let win? If we cater to the flesh, it will win. But if we cater to the Spirit, it will win.

In verse 8, Moses tells Joshua to choose men to fight Amalek while he goes up on the mountain with Aaron and Hur and with the rod of God in his hand. It may sound strange for Moses to tell Joshua to fight Amalek while he went to the top of a mountain to pray. God called Moses, not Joshua. Moses should have been the one going into the valley to fight Amalek and the Amalekites. However, Moses was preparing to teach a valuable lesson to Joshua, Israel, and us.

Some battles are not won in the valley; some battles can only be won on the mountain in prayer. Moses was holding his staff, the instrument of divine power. By holding it up to heaven, he was appealing for God to defend the people. Moses was also in the posture for prayer. He stood with his arms raised up to God. The Israelites generally stood when they prayed, lifting their hands to offer their praises and their petitions up to God.

Something strange happened while Moses was on top of the mountain. As long as Moses' hands were up, Joshua and the men won the battle. But when his arms got tired and fell, the Amalekites won the battle. So, Aaron and Hur held Moses' arms up until the going down of the sun and Israel won the battle. In their first battle outside of Egypt, Moses and the children of Israel got the victory with God's help.

1. How do you react to a crisis?

2. Do you have adverse situations that reoccur in your life just as the Amalekites continued to hound the Israelites for generations? How do you handle them?

3. What battles are you fighting now? What strategies are you using to fight them? Is prayer included in your strategies?

Lord, sometimes I complain before I worship and praise. You've performed many miracles in my life, but sometimes I allow the Marahs to blind me to Your blessings in Elim. Forgive me for not being thankful for what You've done and the battles You've won. In Jesus' name. Amen.

10

Lesson 10
Everyone Needs a Jethro
Exodus 18

Jethro Visits Moses

Over 25 years ago, the late Rev. Dr. Manuel L. Scott exposed me to a book entitled *See Yourself in the Bible*, written by Walter Russell Bowie in 1966. Although the book is dated, it offers significant insights. Bowie challenges his readers to review the life of biblical characters to see whom they identify with in the Bible. However, we often miss pearls of wisdom when we fail to include the stories of biblical characters whose names we rarely hear. In the Exodus narrative, there is an important biblical character who does not receive a lot of press but is responsible for Moses' long tenure as emancipator of Israel: Moses' father-in-law, Jethro.

Some years ago, I scanned the bookshelves at United Lutheran Seminary in Philadelphia, searching for books about Jethro. I looked in George Matheson's four-volume book *Portraits of Bible Men*, John Phillips's book *Exploring People of the Old Testament*, and George Milligan's book *Men of the Bible, Some Lesser-Known Characters*. None of these books or others I perused mentioned, listed, or named Jethro, but the reality is everyone needs a Jethro.

There's no doubt that Moses is the main character in the Book of Exodus. However, Jethro cannot be ignored. Moses was tasked with not only leading God's people out of Egypt and on to the Promised Land, but he was also tasked with instructing the Israelites on what God had to say to them. He was their teacher and their leader.

It was only natural that Moses would be the one the people would count on to settle disputes and to judge on legal disagreements in situations involving property ownership, business dealings, community harmony, and informing the people of God's decrees and laws. But without realizing it, Moses was fast approaching a head-on crash with burnout. He was so taken up with what had developed as a normal routine that he didn't see what was coming. However, God would provide Jethro to give him wise counsel.

Jethro had been keeping tabs on Moses. Verse 1 says, "Jethro, the priest of Midian, Moses' father-in-law, heard of all that God had done for Moses and for his people Israel, how the Lord had brought Israel out of Egypt." Two million people leaving Egypt, crossing the Red Sea, moving southward in the Sinai Peninsula, and defeating the Amalekites was news that could not be contained. Jethro wanted to hear the whole story. In verse 6, he informed Moses that he was coming for a visit and bringing with him Moses' wife, Zipporah, and their two sons, Gershom and Eliezer.

Moses had not seen Jethro for some time. Verse 7 says that Moses rose to greet his father-in-law, as was the custom, bowing down and kissing him. Ordinarily, a great man would wait in his tent to receive a guest, and Moses would have been considered great. God had chosen him to lead the children of Israel. However, Moses left his tent to greet his father-in-law.

Moses' actions were more than a polite ancient Near East custom. Moses' actions demonstrate humility and reverence. He bowed down to Jethro. In the West, such bowing would be of the head only. But in the East, there is a more expressive custom of saluting with the head erect and the body inclined forward, by raising the hand to the heart, mouth, and forehead. The symbolic meaning of this action is like saying, "My heart, my voice, and my brain are all at your service."

Moses not only bowed before Jethro, but he also kissed him. This custom of embraces and kisses among men, though strange to us, was common in the East. It was a sign of friendship, respect, and affection. In Luke 7, when entertained by a Pharisee, Jesus commented on his reception by saying, "Thou gavest me no kiss." Even though Moses was the leader of millions of people, he bowed before Jethro as a sign of humility and kissed him as a sign of respect, friendship, and affection.

In the midst of a busy schedule, Moses took time to share with Jethro all the events that had transpired since he had seen him last. Verse 8 tell us, "Then Moses told his father-in-law all that the Lord had done to Pharaoh and to the Egyptians for Israel's sake, all the hardship that had beset them on the way, and how the

LORD had delivered them." Moses told Jethro about the centuries of bondage that Israel had suffered in Egypt, how they were forced to find their own straw to make bricks. He talked about appearing before Pharaoh for the first time, and of Pharaoh's rejection of God's demands: the plagues, one after the other, the night of the Passover, as the angel of death came through the land.

Moses told Jethro how the Israelites had left Egypt and how God brought them across the Red Sea; protected them in the desert; made bitter water sweet; sent manna and quail from heaven; and delivered them from the Amalekites, giving them victory in their first great battle.

Hearing all that the Lord had done for Israel, Jethro praised God. In verse 11, he proclaims, "Now I know that the LORD is greater than all gods, because he delivered the people from the Egyptians, when they dealt arrogantly with them." Keep the cultural context in mind regarding the phrase "greater than all the gods" because in Jethro's culture there was prolific pagan polytheism, and the people worshiped many gods.

Furthermore, some commentators believe that, at the time, Jethro had not come to faith in the God of Israel. As verse 1 says, he was still the priest of Midian, which assumes that he was still the servant of a pagan god. His unbelief is said to have been confirmed in verse 11, where he says, "Now I know that the LORD is greater than all gods." His words imply that up to now, he wasn't certain that the Lord was greater than all gods. But after he heard Moses' testimony concerning what God had done, he said, now I know that the Lord is greater than all gods.

We who have been redeemed have our own testimony of what God has done in our lives, and someone like Jethro needs to hear it. Our faith account may be the very conversation that will touch the hearts of those God is calling.

The most important thing about Moses' proclamation to Jethro is how thoroughly God-centered it was. It was theocentric, which means it was all about God. We should be sure that our testimony is God-centered. The truth about God disclosed by Moses energized in Jethro a greater sense of the Person of God so that Jethro could relate to God on a more personal and intimate level.

Now the text takes an abrupt turn at verse 13: "The next day Moses sat as judge for the people, while the people stood around him from morning until evening. When Moses' father-in-law saw all that he was doing for the people, he said, 'What is this that you are doing for the people? Why do you sit alone, while all the people stand around you from morning until evening?' " The day after Jethro acknowledged the superiority of God, Moses went out to judge the people. Moses did not take a week off to enjoy his family and fellowship with Jethro. Instead, he was immediately back dealing with disputes. The people were lined up at the designated place to hear from Moses. With a nation composed of nearly two million people, one can imagine that the line was long.

The people came to Moses with matters that needed a decision. They came looking for instructions, a word from God for guidance, and advice on how to handle their disputes. At the end of the day, the long line of waiting Israelites was still there. The people were weary from standing all day, and Moses was exhausted from having had to meet with the people.

Jethro observed Moses as Moses sat and judged all the cases that were brought before him. He was baffled that Moses was trying to do it all by himself. Jethro approached Moses with respect and asked, "What is this that you are doing for the people? Why do you sit alone, while all the people stand around you from morning until evening?" (verse 14). In other words, "Moses, what on earth are you doing?" Moses thought he was declaring God's will for the people, so he tried to justify himself (verses 15-16).

We can't fault Moses for his response; it was the truth. He was not rationalizing. He was not defensive. He simply said, "Look, I've got a big job. I am called of God to be the judge, to serve over these people. They have a series of complaints, and I am the complaint department. They line up, and they have to wait until I can get to them, one by one. It's an enormous job, but somebody has to do it." The work Moses was doing needed to be done, but Moses was stressed and tired.

Moses' stress was honestly earned. He was not lazy. He didn't suffer from one of the seven deadly sins, known as sloth. He was getting into the office before sunup and not leaving until sundown. He was working six days a week with no vacations and no time off. He was the classic workaholic. His fuel tank was empty. He had not only reached his limits; he had exceeded his limits. Now he had to see his limits.

In the nineteenth century, the maritime industry was having a difficult time with ships sinking in heavy seas. English politician Samuel Plimsoll submitted a bill in Parliament insisting that a line be drawn around the outside of the hull on all British ships. When the ships were loaded with freight and reached the level where the line hit the water, the ships were not allowed to load anymore freight. That marking on a ship's hull became known as the Plimsoll Line. We all have a Plimsoll line. We have limits, and if we add anything else to our list, we will sink.

On the outside, Moses looked impressive, but he was burning the candle at both ends, and his wax was almost gone. However, Jethro told Moses, "What you are doing is not good. You will surely wear yourself out, both you and these people with you. For the task is too heavy for you; you cannot do it alone" (verses 17-18).

Jethro was concerned for the people, but he was ultimately concerned about Moses. "You will surely wear yourself out." The Hebrew word for "wearing out" literally means, "to become old" or "to be withered with exhaustion." Moses was growing old before his time, wearing himself out. In essence, Jethro told Moses, "Son, if you keep this pace up and do not make some changes, you are going to wither away."

Could it be that Moses was suffering from what we call a "messiah complex"? In 1988, Carmen Renee wrote a book titled *When Helping You Is Hurting Me*. Renee argues that we can become so caught up in meeting other people's needs that we neglect our own as we operate under a messiah complex. This refers to a state of mind in which people believe they are responsible for saving or assisting others. It's the feeling that we can save the world, carry everyone's burden, and fix everyone problems.

People who work in helping professions—such as pastors, doctors, nurses, counselors, therapists, teachers, and parents—are prone to having a messiah complex. They're always accustomed to rescuing and helping people. There's nothing wrong with helping others, but the people offering help often neglect themselves. While they're trying to rescue others, their own lives may be falling apart.

As a pastor, I often find myself trying to fix everyone's problems, trying to be there for everyone else, because I know God will use me. It's easy for me to get stuck in a messiah complex, feeling as if I need to save everyone by myself. But that's not my job. We don't have the power to save. That's God's job. And the sooner we let go of trying to do that and be everyone's savior, the better it will be because then God finally gets to be God. Our God is bigger, greater, stronger, better, and more capable than we are.

1. Who are the Jethros in your life who have given you wise counsel and constructive criticism when you needed it?

2. When have you stretched yourself too thin? How did you arrive in that space?

3. Have you experienced the messiah complex? What happened?

Father-in-Law Knows Best

Jethro knew Moses inside and out. In Exodus 2, Moses had worked for Jethro in Midian for 40 years. After that many years together, Jethro knew Moses' tendencies, his work habits, and his strengths and weakness. And with the familiarity that only family members or close friends could have, Jethro didn't hold back when he advised Moses: "The task is too heavy for you; you cannot do it alone" (verse 18). That's probably not what Moses wanted to hear. He believed he was just doing his job, being the leader God wanted him to be. But now Jethro was telling him in no uncertain terms that Moses was failing at his job.

Moses' experience is like my own. I, too, am sometimes guilty of trying to do too much. Were it not for the wise counsel from concerned friends, some of our church leaders, colleagues in ministry, and an insightful wife who cares about my well-being, there is a good chance I would not be here today. It's hard to slow down Type A people who have good health along with a lot of energy and drive. However, when a person does too much, works too many hours, and stays at it too many days a week, it begins to show.

Each of us is gifted in particular areas, but when we take on too much, we weaken or dilute our best efforts. The exercise of our highest-priority gifts begins to suffer because we have added too many other things to our list. Soon our priorities get shifted, and our energy gets drained. We lose direction, but we also put ourselves in danger of losing our health and our families.

Jethro pointed out how monumental his task was. Then, in verse 19, he says to Moses, "Now listen to me . . . and all these people will go to their home in peace." Many of us were raised to be problem-solvers, multi-taskers, and go-getters. We believe the saying, "If you want a job done right, do it yourself." Sometimes this is true, but other times it implies that we are the only ones capable of accomplishing a task. Not only does this indicate that we think we're irreplaceable, but it puts us in a no-win situation that can soon become exhausting.

Jethro advised his son-in-law to take a much healthier approach to fulfilling his assignment. Instead of tackling a job alone if he wanted it done right, Moses should have able people to do it, and ask them! In other words, learn how to delegate. Delegation can be a lifesaver, therefore becoming our most important task. It does not entail passing off unwanted responsibilities; instead, it takes place when we empower the right people to accomplish significant tasks with the appropriate direction, support, and accountability.

One of the reasons we sometimes hold so tightly to all the duties we've assigned ourselves is because we have become controlling and want to micromanage everything and everyone. Part of the blessing of learning how to delegate involves us letting go of the need to control everything and trusting God that the work will still get done. President Theodore Roosevelt said that the best executive is the one who has sense enough to pick good people to do what needs to be done and the self-restraint to keep from meddling with them while they do it.

Jethro promised Moses two benefits if he would heed his advice to delegate some of his responsibilities. One, Moses would endure; second, the people would be at peace. In fact, there would be fewer conflicts for Moses to deal with. Moses listened to Jethro and was better because of it. Jethro's impact would not only help Moses to succeed, but it would reach future generations, resulting in a tiered legal system, empowering people to share leadership, raising awareness of burnout, and institutionalizing conflict resolution.

We all need a Jethro, someone a few steps ahead of us who will share their experiences, knowledge, and wisdom. We can read books and research various topics, but there is nothing quite like having someone who is willing to speak life over us and help us to see what we can't see. Jethro reminds those inside and outside the ministry that our task is not to make and keep people dependent upon us, but to equip and empower others. Our job is not to do everything for others, but we are to help others learn how to do things for themselves.

1. When have you taken on too much and become overwhelmed?

2. Have you learned how to delegate? If so, how has that helped you? How does delegation help conquer perfectionism and control issues?

3. How can delegation have a ripple effect in the lives of those you are trying to help?

Reflect and Pray

With so many people to lead, Moses quickly became overwhelmed. He was trying to help over two million people by himself. Although he was only doing his job as leader, he failed to see how he could best position himself not only to help God's people, but to empower others to help themselves. It took a fortuitous visit from his father-in-law, Jethro, to help him to learn the importance of delegation in leadership.

Sometimes we, too, take on more than we can do. We want to help everybody with everything. As virtuous and righteous as that sounds, it can also indicate a deeper problem. We may be suffering from a messiah—or Superman—complex. We're trying to save everyone because we think that we alone are the only ones God is using to do it. We need a Jethro to take us aside lovingly but firmly and give us wise counsel. We need to step back from what we're doing and let God give us vision and discernment. Then we can be a blessing in all the right ways to ourselves as well as to other people.

God, there are times I can't see clearly. I'm stressed and overwhelmed. Give me the wisdom to carry out my assignment in a way that's pleasing to You, not in ways that give me all the glory and attention. Help me to step back and learn to empower those around me to be part of the work of the Kingdom, too. In Jesus' name. Amen.

11

Lesson 11
Experiencing God's Glory
Exodus 33:12-23

God's Presence

On October 17, 1995, twin girls Kyrie and Brielle Jackson were born 12 weeks premature in the Medical Center Hospital in Worcester, Massachusetts. Kyrie—who weighed two pounds, three ounces—made good progress and gained weight. But her sister, Brielle, had breathing problems and gained little weight. In fact, her weight fell under one pound. Her oxygen level was low, her heartbeat was rapid, she was visibly anxious, and her health was deteriorating every day.

On November 12, Brielle went into critical condition. Doctors and nurses worked frantically to stop what they saw as her inevitable death, but nothing they did seemed to work. Brielle's parents feared they might lose one of their daughters. However, one member of the nursing staff had heard of the European practice of co-bedding premature babies.

As a last resort, the nurses put the weaker twin, Brielle, in the same bed as her sister, Kyrie. As soon as the incubator door closed, Brielle snuggled up to Kyrie and calmed down. As she slept, Kyrie wrapped her left arm around her sister. One of the nurses on duty said that the results were immediate and dramatic. As Brielle snuggled up to her sister, her heart rate immediately slowed to normal, her color came back, she visibly relaxed, and she accepted nourishment. The crisis was over, and both babies survived.

Many of us are like Brielle, the weaker twin. We need to be close to God, to experience God, to survive. We need a sense of God's presence to feel alive. When we do not have that presence, our lives seem not to have any meaning, and we begin to waste away. The reality is we are made for God, and we are made for fellowship with God and with one another. When we are isolated and alone, our lives are in trouble, like little Brielle. But our hearts will not fade or die when we are close to God or when we get a sense of God's presence among us. This is where we find Moses.

1. How do you feel when you can't sense God's presence?

2. What happens to cause you to feel far from God?

3. How do you return to a closer relationship with God?

What Were They Thinking?

Our text begins in Exodus 32 with Moses up on the mountain talking with God and the children of Israel down on the plain. When Moses first went up on the mountain, there were flashes of lightning and the sound of thunder. When he came down, his face glowed, and everyone listened as Moses read the Ten Commandments and pledged to obey all the Lord had said. Then Moses went back up the mountain to get more instructions from the Lord. The cloud of the Lord's presence covered the mountain. It was like a devouring fire. Israel was excited as they waited to hear what Moses had to say. They sat at the foot of the mountain and waited—and waited and waited and waited.

They were at a standstill in the desert waiting for Moses on whom they were completely dependent. Moses had been gone for over a month. In faith, they had followed him. In faith, they had committed to obey all the words he said God had given him up on the mountain. In faith, they were waiting on Moses. God had already given the children of Israel the Ten Commandments, and now God was completing the constitutional guidelines that would guarantee their life and liberty for generations to come.

The people had experienced and seen all the signs proving that God was with them: the parting of the Red Sea, the bitter water made sweet, the gift of manna and quail from heaven, and the defeat of the Amalekites. Still, Moses had been gone a long time and, like most of us, they didn't like to wait, especially for a long time. Stress, uncertainty, and anxiety plagued them; and they tossed their faith in God and Moses aside and gave in to their emotions.

Moses was up on Mount Sinai for 40 days. That would be a long time for most of us to wait if we're sitting in the desert with no cellphone, internet, or any form of entertainment to keep us occupied until Moses returned. Israel grew impatient. They confronted Moses' brother, Aaron, who was second in command:

Worshiping the golden calf, as in Exodus 32:1-35, illustration from a Bible card published 1901 by the Providence Lithograph Company.

"We don't know what's happened to Moses. He's been up on that mountain for 40 days. So, you make a god for us to lead us through the wilderness."

In a moment of weakness brought about by their impatience, the people seemed to forget all about God and God's power to deliver and provide for them. Now they wanted Aaron to create a tangible God for them, one they could see and touch. So, they brought their gold to Aaron, who melted it and made an icon of a golden calf, and everyone worshiped it.

But God saw what Israel was doing below and broke the news to Moses that while the two of them had been drawing up the plans for a new sanctuary, the Israelites had decided to make plans of their own. They made for themselves a golden calf and worshiped it and sacrificed to it. They even said, "These are your gods, O Israel, who brought you up out of the land of Egypt!"

Moses knew nothing of what was going on down in the camp of the Israelites, but God knew. This became a demonstration of God's omniscience. *Omniscience* means, "all-knowing" or "knows everything." *Omni* means, "all," and *science* in its original sense means, "knowing." God is all-knowing in the sense that God is aware of the past, present, and future. Nothing takes God by surprise. God knows all that there is to know and all that can be known. Nothing is hidden from God's eyes.

The psalmist affirmed this in Psalm 139 when he wrote, "O Lord, thou hast searched me, and known me.

Thou knowest my downsitting and mine uprising, thou understandest my thought afar off. Thou compassest my path and my lying down, and art acquainted with all my ways. For there is not a word in my tongue, but, lo, O Lord, thou knowest it altogether."

As Moses made his way down the mountain, when he saw what the people and Aaron had done, Moses came to the end of his rope. He had had all he could take. He had been through the conflict in Egypt, the danger of the Red Sea, the trudging through the wilderness, the hunger and thirst, the complaints from the people, and now this. Moses realized that the people he had been leading were not mature enough, strong enough, or committed enough to keep the faith in a time of uncertainty. The first things they did when Moses was out of sight was to disbelieve God's promise, violate God's law, and break God's covenant by making an idol god.

When we fail to wait on God and trust God, we will be tempted to do the same. We will attempt to work things out our own way and in our own time, and soon we will find ourselves turning away from God's precepts and coming up with our own strategies for making life work on our terms. We will bow to the false gods of success and control. We will begin to pay more attention to our occupations than to serving God. We may not be tempted to make a golden calf, but we may be tempted to turn the God who is with us into the kind of god we would like God to be, which is a god of our own making and in our sinful image.

God had been immensely compassionate with Israel, but now it was time for correction. Thus, God dismissed the Israelites with disdain and called them "stiff-necked." *Stiff-necked* is a reference to a mule or an ox that resists the lead rope and refuses to let its master lead it. Instead, it stiffens its neck against the reins. This phrase is one of the Bible's standard ways of referring to the Israelites. What kind of people were they? A stiff-necked people who refused to lower their heads and wear the yoke of obedience to God. This is a dangerous position for anyone to be in. When we become a stiff-necked people, we will always think we are right and never admit when we are wrong.

However, the making of the golden calf wasn't the worst of Israel's indiscretions. Israel failed their test of faith. While Moses was on the mountain for 40 days and 40 nights, Israel needed to wait, have faith, and trust God. This was Israel's chance to prove their faith in God, but they failed. In biblical numerology, the number *40* appears to have been used by God to represent a period of testing, preparation, or judgment.

When circumstances test our faith, we have a choice: create our own golden calf or wait, in faith, on the Lord to provide. If we are committed to our faith in God, then we will and must be tested. It won't be easy. However, as we mature in our faith and persevere through trials, we will develop patience, experience, and hope. Remember, faith doesn't make life easier, it just makes us stronger. If we are experiencing a trial or a test, like the children of Israel did, we must not become impatient, grow weary, faint, and give up. God may not necessarily be disciplining us, but God may be testing us so we can see how strong our faith and trust is in God. A faith that can't be tested is a faith that can't be trusted.

1. When have you been impatient with God's timing?

2. What "golden calves" have you created when you refused to wait on God?

3. How are your golden calves a betrayal of God and a failure of your faith?

Seeing God's Glory

God was angry with the people of Israel, and rightly so. After all God had done for them, they had turned their backs on God again. Moses interceded for the people, though he was angry with them as well. In Chapter 33, it is obvious that God is still angry with Israel. God decided to send them on their way. God was going to allow the Israelites to continue their journey to the Promised Land; but in verse 3, God told them, "Go up to a land flowing with milk and honey; but I will not go up among you, or I would consume you on the way, for you are a stiff-necked people."

The people wanted and needed God to live close to them so they could survive, just as Brielle needed her sister, Kyrie, close to her to survive. But God was unwilling to do so because of Israel's sin. God had been drawing Israel closer. God had answered their prayers and provided for their needs. God had taught them the Law. God had made plans to build a home, a dwelling place, in the middle of their camp. God was totally committed to this relationship, but Israel was loosening the bond with their sinful idolatry.

God wants to fill our lives and be present with us; but when we carry other things around with us, pursuing them by day and thinking about them at night, there is no room left for God. Instead of going with Israel personally to the Promised Land, God told them He would send an angel. In verses 1-6, God offers Moses everything He promised to Abraham, Isaac, and Jacob, including military success, peace, prosperity, abundance, land, security, safety, and freedom from fear, with no strings attached. God said, "You'll have all these things, but you won't have me, and you won't have my presence. I'll send an angel instead."

Moses knew the people could not make it without God's presence. So, Moses set up the tent of meeting, which was a special place where he met with God. There, Moses interceded once again for the people. In verses 14-15, God and Moses have a conversation: "He said, 'My presence will go with you, and I will give you rest.' If your presence will not go, do not carry us up from here."

God offered Moses and Israel an angel to go with them, military success, prosperity, land, security, safety, and more, and Moses boldly said no. Moses told God, "That's not enough! If your presence will not go with me, do not bring us up from here." This may seem contradictory to what God had just said in verse 14: "My presence will go with you, and I will give you rest." In verse 15, it seems as if Moses doesn't even hear what God has just said. Moses said, "If your presence will not go with me, do not bring us up from here." The truth is Moses was listening to what God said in verse 14. God told Moses, "My presence is going to go with you, Moses. I'm going to have a personal relationship with you. I'm going to save you, but not with the Israelites."

Moses rightly understood that ultimately God was saying, "I'm going to give Israel all the land and peace and prosperity and military success that they could ask for, but I'm going to let them go their own way. I'm not going with them because of their sin. If they do not want a relationship with me, I'm going to honor their wishes."

When Moses said, "If you don't go, we won't go," he was not resorting to blackmail. He had a serious reason for saying this. Moses knew that Israel needed God. Moses was saying, "They need You, God, infinitely more than they need me, the land that You promised them, the peace and prosperity, the financial security, or the military success that You are promising them now. Even though You are offering to take care of me and give me everything I could want, as well as Your presence, it's not enough unless You do the same for them!"

Moses then boldly pleaded in verse 16: "For how shall it be known that I have found favour in your sight, I and your people, unless you go with us? In this way, we shall be distinct, I and your people, from every people on the face of the earth." What was distinct about the Israelites? It was not their land, because they didn't have any land yet. It was not their wealth, because other nations had more treasure. It was not their culture, because they had been living in enslavement. It was not their righteousness, because they could not keep even the most basic commandments.

The only thing the Israelites had going for them was their relationship with God. Other nations would only know that God was their God if God stayed in their midst. Without the Lord's presence, life is futile and empty. We cannot do anything effectively if the Lord does not go with us. Our efforts, intentions, and endeavors, regardless of how valid they are, will be in vain.

In verse 17, the Lord says to Moses, "I will do the very thing that you have asked; for you have found favour in my sight, and I know you by name." At this point, most people would have been satisfied. God told Moses that his prayer request would be granted. But Moses wanted more. Thus, he made an outrageous and audacious request. In verse 18, Moses says, "Show me your glory, I pray."

Moses had already seen something of God's glory. He caught his first glimpse at the burning bush, which blazed with fire but was not consumed. He received another glimpse with the 70 elders who witnessed or got a sense of God. Then he was covered with glory when he went to the mountaintop and entered the cloud of God's presence. He saw God's glory again at the tent of meeting, where the pillar of cloud descended from heaven.

But somehow Moses knew there was still more to see. He wanted a full revelation of God's glory, a visible display of the essential quality of God's being. Thus, he asked God to show him the glory of God. What made Moses' request outrageous is that Moses wanted to, in some way, erase the line between immortal God and mortal beings. He wanted to tear down all walls that separated men and women from God. He wanted complete and unlimited access to the Holy of Holies, to the soul of God. Why would Moses make such an outrageous request?

Maybe it was because Moses wanted to know God more intimately. What better way to know God than to see a total revelation of God's glory? Whatever Moses' reasons for asking, he wanted to have a personal encounter with the glory of God. God responded, "I will make all my goodness pass before you." This was a yes-and-no answer. God was willing to reveal transcendent goodness to Moses. God was willing to announce the sacred divine name, and God was willing to reveal the sovereign grace of God's mercy and compassion.

What God was not willing to do was to allow Moses to gaze upon the glory of God. In other words, God would not give Moses a direct perception of God's divine being. God's goodness would pass by, but the fullness of God's glory would not be seen at all. The reason for this restriction was simple.

If Moses were to see a complete revelation of God's eternal being, it would be so overwhelming it would destroy him. God is absolute and perfect. Moses was a finite, fallen creature; as such, he could not see God and live. No one can. Theologian Rudolph Otto wonderfully captures the essence of God's holiness in the Latin phrase *mysterium tremendum*, meaning that God's holiness or glory is a mystery that is at once terrifying and fascinating. God was willing to show as much of the glory of God as Moses could bear, but there were limits.

Some things are beyond our capacity to know. Moses could not see God's absolute character. He could not see God's face and live. God's face represents the display of God's glory. God does not have a literal face; God is Spirit. Neither does God have arms, feet, legs, hands, or other body parts. The Scriptures uses what are known as anthropomorphic expressions to teach our finite minds truths about our infinite God. God uses elementary terms to teach us the attributes of God. God brings it down to our level so we can understand. This reminds us that God is incompressible, that God dwells in unapproachable light.

The angels themselves around the throne shield their eyes from the glory of God. God's glory is simply too much for men and women to handle. Moses would have died if he had looked at God's face, because that would have erased all boundaries between Moses and God. Furthermore, for God to tell Moses he could only look at God's back does not mean that Moses could look at the back of God's pants as opposed to the front of God's pants. It meant that Moses could have access to God, but not unlimited access. He could have a relationship with God, but it would be as unequals.

God is always going to be God, and humans are always going to be humans. We cannot erase the line. To do so would mean death and annihilation. It would mean the end to humanity. The denial of Moses' request to see the face of God was for Moses' own good. Only God knows how to handle the power within God's grasp. Only God can harness the glory of God's presence in a way that won't annihilate us.

Moses' experience is a reminder to all that we are not equal with God. We are partners but unequal partners. We can have a conversation with God, but we do not dictate to God. We can try to challenge God, but God is free to put us in our place whenever God wants.

Moses could not see God fully; he could see only God's back, the "afterglow of the effulgence of His presence,"[1] as Robert Alter describes it. God told Moses that as the glory of God passed by, he would place Moses in a cleft of a rock, cover Moses with the hand of God, so that Moses would be under the shadow of

God's care. God would shield Moses from the radiance of God's glory.

A cleft is a narrow space or a split. This would have put the rock under Moses' feet, behind his back, and on either side of him. Moses would be wedged into this rock, which would hold him in place and provide a stable base. From that vantage point, he would behold the back of God's glory. In essence, God placed Moses in the cleft of a rock so Moses would be protected by God from God.

We want to know, understand, and see God. We might catch only glimpses of God's presence, hear only snippets of God's voice, feel only the breeze of God's touch, for God encounters us on God's terms, not ours. We may see only God's backside, but it's enough. It's enough for faith, strength, and hope. There is a mystery to God we can never penetrate. However, even in that mystery, God reaches out to us. We can experience God's presence and glory, even if it seems only a fleeting glimpse.

Whatever Moses saw when he saw God's back, it was enough to sustain him as he continued his long journey toward the Promised Land after this experience. In the twists and turns of our lives, in the exhilarating but frustrating work of ministry, God will give us just enough presence to remind us that we are not alone.

Wherever life leads us, God will go with us to the end, but it will only be after death that we will see God's glory directly. And in that moment, every eye will see God; every ear will hear God. Every saint's hand will touch God; every lip will praise God. Every mouth will worship God; and every knee will bow, of things in heaven, and things in earth, and things under the earth; and every tongue will confess that Jesus Christ is Lord, to the glory of God the Father.

But for now, as Paul writes in 1 Corinthians, "Now we see in a mirror, dimly, but then we will see face to face. Now I know only in part; then I will know fully, even as I have been fully known." I want to experience God's glory, but for now, as Paul says, we will know only in part. But one day, there will come a time when we will see God, face to face.

1. Was Moses' request to see God unreasonable? Why or why not?

2. When have you seen God's glory?

3. If you've seen God's glory, did it change you? If so, how?

Reflect and Pray

We shouldn't be surprised at the Israelites' behavior as they waited for Moses to descend Mount Sinai. We, too, struggle with impatience, especially when we're waiting on God's timing. We may not melt down a pile of gold and make a golden calf, but we have other forms of "golden calves" in our lives that we worship. Without realizing it, we sometimes worship our careers, money, position, power, people we look up to (or idolize), our children, status, our influence on social media, sex, and even our pain. We can make idols of any of these things and so much more and put them in God's rightful place. But God is not pleased with competing gods or idols. God will not share God's glory with any other god.

Instead of trying to fill the void with other people or other things, we should allow God to be Lord of our lives. We should long to see and experience as much of God's glory as God will allow. When Moses saw only the "hinder parts" of God, he was noticeably changed. And we can be changed, too. Our lives will never be the same.

Lord, sometimes I grow impatient waiting for You. In those in-between times, I'm tempted to make my own version of the golden calf. Forgive me for putting other gods before You, and help me long for Your glory alone. Reveal Yourself to me in a real and meaningful way, and change my life forever. In Jesus' name. Amen.

---

[1] *The Five Books of Moses: A Translation with Commentary*, by Robert Alter (W. W. Norton and Company, 2008); page 506.

12

Lesson 12
The Tragedy of a Missed Opportunity
Numbers 13:13-33; 14:1-12; 20:1-12

If Only I Had Known

There are times when we look back on certain events that occurred in our lives, and all we can think is, *I blew it*. I assume that is what John Antioco says to himself every time he remembers a meeting he had in Dallas, Texas, in September 2000. Antioco was the CEO of a company that ruled the video world, Blockbuster Video. For much of the 1980s and 1990s, Blockbuster was the unrivaled champion of the video rental market, with people flocking to their stores every week and searching the shelves for the latest Hollywood releases. So secure was Blockbuster's market dominance throughout the 1990s that the video chain barely batted an eye when an upstart internet company began making waves with their video-by-mail service.

In his book titled *That Will Never Work*, Netflix cofounder Marc Randolph describes the meeting in Dallas with Antioco, along with Netflix cofounder Reed Hastings and its chief financial officer Barry McCarthy. At the time, Netflix was in financial trouble and offered Blockbuster the chance to buy the company.

But Antioco didn't even bother to consider the possibility. In fact, he nearly laughed in the faces of Netflix's cofounders when they offered to sell their fledgling company to the video giant for the bargain basement price of $50 million. Antioco saw the offer as a big joke. Blockbuster did not accept Netflix's offer or make a serious counteroffer. In his book, Randolph writes, "The meeting went downhill pretty quickly, and it was a long, quiet ride back to the airport."[1]

Ten years later, Blockbuster filed for bankruptcy, and its last stores in Alaska closed in July 2018. However, Netflix's revenue is $5.768 billion, has slightly more than 203 million subscribers, and is available for streaming in over 190 countries. Blockbuster's corporate leaders must cringe when they think back on the offer made to them in 2000. It was the tragedy of a missed opportunity.

This is not the first time that a company missed out on an opportunity. Verizon shunned Apple for the first model of the iPhone, Comcast didn't buy Disney, Friendster refused Google, AOL merged with Time-Warner instead of AT&T, and Yahoo missed its chance to buy Google and Facebook. These are the tragedies of missed opportunities, proving that life is a series of opportunities offered and choices faced.

Antioco, the former CEO of Blockbuster, has probably revisited that meeting in his mind and thought, *If I could do it all over again, I would do things differently.* Through his misfortune, however, he learned that there are some opportunities that only come once in a lifetime and can never be recaptured. This is where a vast number of people find themselves. There are people struggling with a bad decision made years ago, the fruit of which is still evidenced in their lives. We all know something about missed opportunities, about choosing the wrong path when a great opportunity presented itself.

1. Do you have regrets around decisions you've made? If so, what are they?

2. How did those decisions affect your future?

3. Were you able to recover from any missed opportunities? If so, how?

Missing Out Because of Fear

In our text today, Moses continues to lead the children of Israel toward the Promised Land. The Israelites had been migrating for about 40 years from Egypt to Canaan. The Lord faithfully brought Israel out of Egyptian bondage and through the wilderness, and now the land of Canaan was right in front of them, a land flowing with milk and honey. At long last, a dream was about to meet reality; the Promised Land was no longer a place of imagination. Rather, it had become a real and tangible site filled with other people, vegetation, wildlife, and fortified construction.

Israel was standing at the intersection of opportunity and choice. The Lord spoke to Moses after they had left Hazeroth and settled in the Paran desert. God ordered Moses to send 12 spies to explore the land of Canaan.

Biblical numbers carry symbolic significance. The number *12* stands out as one of the most prominent in Scripture. The number *12* appears numerous times throughout the Bible. It is a number that typically means perfection or authority often used in a context of government. Jacob had 12 sons, who formed the 12 tribes of Israel. Solomon appointed 12 district governors over Israel. When Israel returned after their captivity, Ezra set apart 12 priests. There are 12 historical books in the bible and 12 minor prophets. Jesus chose 12 disciples, and later the disciples replaced Judas Iscariot with Matthias to keep the number at 12 to show the perfection and authority of those who followed Jesus.

The New Jerusalem that descends out of heaven has 12 gates, which are made of pearl and manned by 12 angels, and the walls of the city of New Jerusalem have 12 foundations. We have 12 months to complete a year. Thus, the number *12* is considered a perfect number in that it symbolizes God's power and authority, as well as a perfect governmental foundation, and the nation of Israel as a whole.

Moses responded to God's command and sent 12 spies: one person from the tribes of Reuben, Simeon, Judah,

Issachar, Ephraim, Benjamin, Zebulun, Manasseh, Dan, Asher, Naphtali, and Gad. One man from each of the tribes of Israel was to serve as a representative in this exploratory group. It was the responsibility of this group to survey the land and bring back a feasibility report. They were being sent by Moses to determine the best routes, the kind of people they would encounter, and the cities they would inherit.

The goal of their mission was not to decide whether to enter the land. The Lord had already reminded them in Numbers 13:1 that the land was being given to them; it was theirs. All they had to do was receive it as a gift, see that what God said was true, and possess the land.

For 40 days, the exploratory group thoroughly investigated the land and found it to be fertile, rich with possibilities, and great potential. To demonstrate the fertility of the land, they "cut down from there a branch with a single cluster of grapes, and they carried it on a pole between two of them. They also brought some pomegranates and figs" (verse 23). They did this to give evidence of the land's productivity. But when it came to making a report to Aaron and Moses and the congregation, the group had a difference of opinion.

"At the end of forty days they returned from spying out the land. And they came to Moses and Aaron and to all the congregation of the Israelites in the wilderness of Paran, at Kadesh; they brought back word to them and to all the congregation, and showed them the fruit of the land. And they told him, 'We came to the land to which you sent us; it flows with milk and honey, and this is its fruit. Yet the people who live in the land are strong, and the towns are fortified and very large; and besides, we saw the descendants of Anak there. The Amalekites live in the land of the Negeb; the Hittites, the Jebusites, and the Amorites live in the hill country; and the Canaanites live by the sea, and along the Jordan'" (verses 25-29).

All 12 group members saw the same thing. Each saw the fertile ground, the productivity of the land, the huge clusters of grapes, the giants, and the descendants of Anak. They saw the Amalekites, the Hittites, the Jebusites, the Amorites, and the Canaanites. Each member of the group saw the possibilities, and all 12 spies brought back the word that the land was as God had said. The report was good; it was undeniable that there were blessings ahead if Moses and the children of Israel would cross over and take it. However, ten members of the group gave a negative report, while two members, Joshua and Caleb, gave a positive report.

These ten committee members were not giving false information. They were telling the truth. There were giants in the land. But if we are going to claim anything that God has for us, if we are going to take advantage of the opportunities before us, there are going to be giants in the land. It would hardly be worth the shout after we gained the victory if we didn't have any giants to face while on our way to our promised land.

After the spies' report, the people went into a frenzy. There was bitterness, disappointment, and even sobbing. Moses called the people to order. They still had another report to hear. It was with the utmost difficulty that two young men, Caleb and Joshua, stood to give the minority report. The people who did not want to progress were probably looking at them with smirks on their faces. But Joshua and Caleb realized that this was a great opportunity, one that might never come their way again. However, the people decided to adopt the recommendation of the ten. The voice of the majority prevailed while the lone voice of Joshua and Caleb was silenced by practicality and fear.

It is easy to come up with excuses and justify why we need to postpone our mission. The longer we fill our heads with rationalizations and empty excuses, the less time we will have to act. But there is never a perfect time to act other than now. If we keep putting it off, by this time next year, we will have a lot more excuses. Most of us live with the illusion that we will always have tomorrow to do today's work.

Chapter 14 tells us that the people lifted their voices, cried out, and murmured against Moses and Aaron. This act of murmuring was far more than complaining or grumbling. It was more like a parliamentary vote of no confidence because they no longer trusted Moses and wanted to choose a new leader and go back to Egypt. They accused God of not allowing them to die in Egypt or in the wilderness or to return to Egypt to live. They said that God brought them to a foreign land to fall by the sword and their families to be plundered.

The people were willing to give up the chance of a lifetime. What caused them, and us, to miss out on great opportunities that would result in being blessed? Fear and doubt, which comes from having a grasshopper mentality. The Israelites should have surged forward with joy. They should have claimed all the abundance and fulfillment God wanted them to have. But after all they had been through, they couldn't take a stand against fear. We may be at the threshold of God's greatest promise for us, but we will never claim the blessings of God if we allow fear to dominate us.

The ten spies made a revealing statement: "There we saw the Nephilim [the Anakites came from the Nephilim]; and to ourselves we seemed like grasshoppers, and so we seemed to them'" (13:33). The Anakites, who were also descendants from the Nephilim, were a formidable race of giants, warlike people who occupied the lands of southern Israel near Hebron. The Anakites were giants who were to be feared, but the Canaanites were there, and they were not giants.

Facts are important, but all too often they overshadow the power and greatness of God. We should not disregard or ignore facts in every case, or in any case, but there are times when faith must overrule facts.

For the ten spies, the threat of giants outweighed the blessing God had waiting for them. They decided to postpone the blessing because of fear and their lack of trust in God to safely deliver them into the Promised Land. Unbelief always waits for a convenient moment. But when we walk with God, there are few if any convenient moments. We must go for what we know and trust God at His word.

There will be giants in our lives, and a grasshopper mentality will not help us knock down those giants. God never promised us that there will not be adversity, but God has promised to give us the power we need to accomplish every goal, every dream, and every opportunity He plants before us. All the ten spies had to do was trust God, who casts out all fear. All Israel had to do was possess the land.

Thank God for Joshua and Caleb, who refused to miss out on a great opportunity. They were not controlled by fear, but rather faith. "The land that we went through as spies is an exceedingly good land. If the LORD is pleased with us, he will bring us into this land and give it to us, a land that flows with milk and honey" (14:7-8). They saw its fruit, they saw that the land flowed with milk and honey, and they saw the enemies in the land. They knew it wasn't going to be easy and that there were going to be obstacles, but they also saw God and knew that God was bigger than any giant that was in their way. And at the moment of opportunity, Joshua and Caleb said, "Let's go and take the land, for if God is with us, He will lead us, and He will guide us."

God was so angry at Israel's decision that God vowed that no one 20 years of age or older would enter the land of promise (Numbers 14:29-30). God made the adults wander in the wilderness for 40 years. A year for each day the exploratory group was in Canaan.

Everyone in that present generation died 21 miles from the Promised Land. They were so close to their blessing, but because of fear, they never stepped foot in the Promised Land. They stood face to face with God, who offered them the land of their hopes; but instead of taking what God had given, they turned their backs and walked away. Theirs was the tragedy of a missed opportunity. God cannot give us what we do not want and what we will not take.

Years ago, essayist Frank Boreham wrote *The Glory of a Lone Black Bird*. Boreham wrote about a black bird that overcame its fears to go into a garden where there was a scarecrow and eat some berries. What fascinated Boreham was that up in the trees and up on the wires were a lot of birds despising that one lone bird that was in the garden. Boreham said he began to talk to those birds that were in the trees and on the wires.

"Hey birds, have you had your breakfast this morning?"

The birds said, "No."

"Are you hungry?"

"Yes."

"Is there anything wrong with the fruit in that garden down there that you are looking at?"

"No, there's nothing wrong with that fruit. That's good fruit down there."

But there was that one bird in the garden just having a good time. Boreham asked, "If there's nothing wrong with the fruit, then why don't you go down in the garden and get some fruit since you haven't had your breakfast?"

"Because of that floppy thing down there in the middle of the garden with those straws in it and that hat on his head," the birds said, referring to the scarecrow.

Then Boreham asked his readers, "Now don't those birds remind you of people? How many scarecrows have kept us out of gardens that God intended us to be in? How many blessings has God placed before us, but because there was a scarecrow or a giant there, we did not take the opportunity to possess those blessings? And now we look back with regret on what we could have had, and it has become for us the tragedy of a missed opportunity.

1. What opportunities have you missed because of fear?

2. When have you had the courage of Joshua and Caleb? When have you been fearful like the ten spies?

3. How can you work on overcoming fear and doubt so that you can partake of all that God has for you?

Stumbling at the Finish Line

An Ironman Triathlon is a series of long-distance races organized by the World Triathlon Corporation. It consists of a 2.4-mile swim, a 112-mile bicycle ride, and a 26.2-mile run. It is widely considered one of the most difficult one-day sporting events in the world. In 1997, Austrian Chris Legh participated in the Ironman World Championship in Kailua-Kona, Hawaii.

Ideally, athletes would start exercising weeks before a triathlon. They would be adequately hydrated and drink enough during exercise or refuel immediately after finishing to replace fluid lost while sweating. Two days before the race, Chris Legh changed his regimen and diet. He eliminated fiber, ate simpler carbohydrates that break down quicker for easier-to-access energy, and curbed his protein intake to lower his chances of gastrointestinal distress.

The morning of the race, Legh consumed only simple carbohydrates, fluids, and electrolytes. After finishing the 2.4-mile swim, Legh started the 112-mile bicycling segment about six minutes behind the leaders. However, he caught up with them, and there were only four people left, including Legh.

When he came to the last leg of the full marathon, 26.2 miles of running, Legh thought that if he just closed his eyes and ran, he would make it to the end, and he would be all right. He was in fifth place but obviously struggling. He could barely stand, and he staggered from side to side. Legh was just 50 yards from the finish line when his legs buckled underneath him. He couldn't even crawl. Eventually, he was carried away on a stretcher without finishing the race.

Legh was so dehydrated that part of his large intestine died and had to be surgically removed; it nearly cost him his life. This elite triathlete had endured almost all the triathlon, and was strides away from finishing, but his run became a stagger, then a crawl. Finally, he collapsed, stumbling at the finish line.

There are people who have prepared themselves to have a successful life and a successful end to life only to stumble at the finish line. Right before the start of life's race, like Chris Legh, they feel pretty good. They have waited a long time for this day, and it's finally here. Then the race starts. All those months of training are finally going to pay off. However, after a couple of miles, they are out of breath. Along with pain and fatigue, doubt and fear begin to creep in, and they stumble at the finish line.

It is said that only 30-35 percent of the people in the Bible finished well. Noah responded to God with great faith, building an ark, despite being laughed at and years of waiting for it to rain. But his story ends with him lying drunk and disgraced in his tent. Jehu had a great start in life. He was chosen by God and anointed by Elisha to be king of Israel. But near the end of his life, Jehu was not careful to walk in the law of the Lord with all his heart and did not turn from sin. Solomon, who had extraordinary wisdom and brought unprecedented prosperity to Israel, allowed his many wives to turn his heart to idolatry. Noah, Jehu, Solomon, and so many others stumbled at the finish line.

Past faithfulness and obedience do not guarantee future faithfulness and obedience. Even a lifetime of walking with God does not ensure that we will finish well. Our text today is the story of one of the greatest men of God in history stumbling near the finish line.

Everyone knows how *Romeo and Juliet* ends, but people still cry when the star-crossed lovers die. Everyone knows how the film *Lady Sings the Blues* plays out, but people still cry at its sad ending. We know how *Cooley High* ends, but we still cry when Cochise dies. The same is true when we read Numbers 20. Many of us have heard about or read this story numerous times, but we are still upset, angry, and baffled that just before Moses enters the Promised Land, he is denied admission.

By the time we get to Numbers 20, only a few of the old generation remains. A new generation of Israelites had emerged, most of whom did not witness the miracles of the Exodus nor the awesome experience of revelation at Sinai. However, this new generation was poised to enter the Promise Land.

Thirty-eight years had elapsed since Moses sent 12 spies from Kadesh to Canaan to survey the land of promise. At the end of 38 years, the Israelites returned to the wilderness of Zin and Kadesh. God had previously judged the older generation of Israelites for unbelief and informed them that they would not enter the

Promised Land. That generation had pretty much died off, and only those who were 20 years old or younger would enter the Promised Land. The only named survivors of the previous generation were Miriam, Aaron, Moses, Joshua, and Caleb.

However, we are told in verse 1, "The Israelites, the whole congregation, came into the wilderness of Zin in the first month, and the people stayed in Kadesh. Miriam died there, and was buried there." Miriam, Moses' sister, was the principal woman in the story of the Exodus from Egypt and Israel's life in the wilderness. In contrast to the longer reports of the deaths of Aaron and of Moses, the barely one-sentence statement concerning the death and burial of Miriam seems unfair. It seems unfair that Miriam's death and burial is reported with such simple reverence. It announces Miriam's death and place of burial but moves immediately to the community complaining.

The statement's brevity with no reference to a period of mourning indicates Miriam's lesser status in the tradition in comparison with her two brothers. More should be said about Miriam. She was a leader among the Israelites, a prophetess and a songstress, a sister of the divinely chosen high priest and prophetic leader of Israel who demonstrated her compassionate character soon after Moses was born. She was the first heroine and the first to be called prophetess. She should have been mourned.

After we are told of Miriam's death, verse 2 says, "Now there was no water for the congregation; so they gathered together against Moses and against Aaron." There were two "water from the rock" events that serve as bookends for the 40 years of wandering in the wilderness. The water episode we read about in Exodus 17 took place immediately after the miraculous crossing of the Red Sea. This water episode in Numbers took place 38 years later, and this narrative is entirely different from the previous occasion.

The people in this account were not simply thirsty for water, as the term for "thirst" does not appear in this narrative at all. Instead, they immediately questioned the whole purpose of the mission. "The people quarreled with Moses and said, 'Would that we had died when our kindred died before the Lord! Why have you brought the assembly of the Lord into this wilderness for us and our livestock to die here? Why have you brought us up out of Egypt, to bring us to this wretched place? It is no place for grain, or figs, or vines, or pomegranates; and there is no water to drink'" (verses 3-5)

The complaint about the water was an afterthought. There was an underlying problem that was bigger than grain, figs, vines, pomegranates, and water. That problem was a lack of faith and trust in God. The reason many of us fail to place our trust in God, like Israel, is due to us focusing on our current situation and not the promises of God.

Life is not predictable. There are ups and downs, twist and turns, along the way. When times are good, it can appear to be easy to place our faith and trust in God. But when times are difficult, or when, like Israel, we are wondering why God has us in a certain place, it is even more important that we place our faith and trust in God.

Israel frequently recalled the luxurious meals of Egypt or visualized the attractive diet of Canaan and saw both in stark contrast to their barren wilderness experience. When we constantly long for what we want, it can cause us to ignore or forget what we have received and forget all that God has done for us. Israel seemed to have forgotten God's mighty acts of deliverance. They ignored the daily evidence of God's presence and the nightly assurance of God's protection. They failed to remember God's unfailing gift of food, the ready supply of necessary water, and the restful locations where they enjoyed shelter.

The people marginalized God's immense kindness in keeping them free from sickness and disease, even protecting their feet from discomfort and their clothing from wearing out. During those long years in the desert, they did not lack anything, but they were not remotely grateful. The whole point of remembering or looking back is to reflect on God's power in the past to increase our faith and trust in God in the present. For when we look back on life, we can see that when things were at their worst, God was at God's best.

Yesterday's powerful display of God's power became old news to the new generation. They could not live off the past generation's experiences with God. Without a new display of divine power, God's miracles would swiftly become a thing of the past. They needed a fresh move of God if they were going to be steadfast in the face of their lack of resources. Their urgency, anger, and complaint toward Moses for bringing them out of Egypt into an arid wilderness caused Moses to listen to their complaints until he could bear it no longer. Moses and Aaron went from the company of a disgruntled people into the presence of God.

They acknowledged God's holiness as "they fell on their faces, and the glory of the Lord appeared to them" (verse 6). Then we read in verses 7-8, "The Lord spoke to Moses, saying: Take the staff, and assemble the congregation, you and your brother Aaron, and command the rock before their eyes to yield its water. Thus you shall bring water out of the rock for them; thus you shall provide drink for the congregation and their livestock."

God spoke to Moses and Aaron and gave them specific instructions. God emphasized that the entire assembly must witness the event. Moreover, the phrase in verse 8 in which God told Moses to "take the staff, and assemble the congregation" and then told Moses and Aaron to "command the rock before their eyes to yield its water," clearly echoes this instruction. It will be emphasized again in verse 12, when God tells Moses that he did not trust in God "to show my holiness before the eyes of the Israelites."

Moses went as God commanded him, but when he spoke to the people, it appears that Moses was angry. According to verses 9-10, "Moses took the staff from before the Lord, as he had commanded him. Moses and Aaron gathered the assembly together before the rock, and he said to them, 'Listen, you rebels, shall we bring water for you out of this rock?' " Moses did not do exactly as the Lord commanded. Instead of speaking to the rock, Moses spoke to the people and called them rebels. We are told in verse 10, he "lifted up his hand and struck the rock twice with his staff." Not once but twice.

If we're honest, we will acknowledge that while Moses' reaction toward the people was wrong and we cannot justify it, we can understand it. Moses had been doing his job for at least 38 years. He was an elderly man. He had waited a long time to enter the Promised Land, and the people he had been leading had been extremely difficult. Nowhere do we read that they came to Moses and said, "Moses, you are doing a wonderful job. Keep up the good work. You have our support." Instead, all they did was complain, murmur, quarrel, and grumble.

Think about what it must have been like for Moses to stutter step in Egypt as he grasped for premature leadership, only to spend 40 years living like a sheepherder as a result. Then he was called out of retirement to lead the Exodus, only to inherit a multitude of complaining people. After almost 40 years, Moses was approaching the finish line, but his patience had come to an end. He was angry, and it got the best of him. For 38 years, he had let it build and build. He had a mental file card of every little thing that the people had done; and at this moment in their travels, it had built up until he could not control himself any longer.

Instead of acknowledging the people's need for food and water, Moses lashed out at them. He gave vent to his frustrations and projected his feelings of inadequacy and helplessness on them. He overreacted to their complaint. He refused to do what God commanded, insulted the people, boasted a bit about his power, and struck the rock instead of speaking to it. Decades of work, long-term suffering and sacrifice, endurance right up to the near final moment, resulted in Moses stumbling at the finish line.

Thus, verse 12 says, "The LORD said to Moses and Aaron, 'Because you did not trust in me, to show my holiness before the eyes of the Israelites, therefore you shall not bring this assembly into the land that I have given them.'" The failure of Moses to lead God's people into the Promised Land because of this one mistake sounds harsh. Every time I read this verse, I approach it as if, when I get to verse 12, the wording will change, and I will read of Moses receiving a lighter sentence, allowing him to enter the Promised Land.

It seems so unfair. Moses' disqualification from entry into the Promised Land left those who loved him with a sense of frustration and wonder. What exactly was Moses' sin, and why was he punished so severely? Was it only his anger, or was it disobedience? Numerous attempts to make sense of this misfortune have troubled and perplexed classical, medieval, modern, and post-modern commentators and scholars.

In verse 1, we are told that Miriam died. On the surface, it appears that Moses and Aaron had little time to grieve their sister. People cope with grief in various ways, as grief can look different for each of us, but we all grieve. Some go through the five stages of grief as outlined by Elisabeth Kübler-Ross. Some need to move on as quickly as possible, turning with intensity of purpose to whatever task readily presents itself, getting back to school or the office. They respond as the Israelites did to Miriam's death, ready to get on with life instead of quieting into the stillness of being. Others respond in anger, lashing out at those who remain alive, as it appears Moses and Aaron did with Israel. Or some can find no outlet for their grief and, like Moses, strike out against a rock.

Moses loved his only sister, Miriam; she meant a great deal to him. He owed his very life to her. Moses could not fail to appreciate Miriam's role as her presence framed his life. She guarded him at birth and exulted with him in song and dance on the other side of the Red Sea. The love Moses had for Miriam was further demonstrated when she was struck with leprosy after she challenged Moses' marriage and authority. Appalled by what he saw affecting his beloved sister, Moses cried out for the Lord to heal her, and the Lord answered his prayer. What effect Miriam's death had on Moses' actions, one can only speculate. But perhaps her death caused Moses to enter a period of depression, anger, or despair, which might have led him to respond so negatively to the people.

Note how important it was to God that Moses speak to the rock in the presence of the entire assembly. God emphasized that the entire assembly was to witness Moses speaking to a rock. As Rabbi Helfgot notes, Moses' error was not merely a failure to obey God's command; it also was a failure of leadership.

It was not only the sin and its severity that caused Moses to lose the privilege of leadership. Moses striking the rock instead of speaking to it revealed that he was not a leader who could address the concerns and crises of the new generation. It was clear that he was still tied to methods and perspectives of leadership that, though proper for the needs and concerns of the former generation that left Egypt, were ineffective and inappropriate for this new generation.

Moses was faced with a new reality that required a different reaction. His inability to respond to this challenge was a revealing litmus test that the time had come to pave the way for a new leader who would continue the mission. Moses demonstrated that he was not capable to lead this new generation, whom God wanted to wean from one kind of perception to another, from dependence on the visible and tangible that the former generation was used to, to reliance on speech in connecting with God, which the new generation would become accustomed to.

Moses stumbled at the finish line. He was halted on the doorstep of the Promised Land, a place he could only gaze at from afar but could not enter. During those last days of his life, Moses probably wished he could go back and finish his race without stumbling. If so, he would have given almost anything, if not everything, to relive the incident at the rock. He would have cried out for God to help him control his anger.

But Moses couldn't go back, and neither can we. Once we start this journey, this Christian race, we can't go back and change the mistakes we have made in life. We must live with the consequences of our words and our actions. However, we can be forgiven and have our sins blotted out of our record by the blood of Christ.

1. What regrets do you have that you wish you could go back in life and change?

2. How does the sad end to Moses' story speak to you?

3. How can you ensure that you won't stumble at the finish line?

Reflect and Pray

As we near the end of Moses' story, we begin to see the toll that leadership has taken on him. We know he was a great leader, but he wasn't without his flaws. But these flaws were not all self-inflicted. Moses had spent the latter third of his life leading several million people who grumbled and complained more than they were thankful. And most of their anger was directed toward God or Moses. If they weren't romanticizing their time in Egypt, they were complaining about the food and water or the weather in the wilderness. And then they refused to enter the Promised Land because of fear and doubt. No wonder Moses' anger boiled over!

But if we are going to finish well and not stumble before we can cross the finish line, we can't let the fear, doubt, ungratefulness, complaining, criticism, and ignorance of others cause us to miss our greatest opportunities, and we can't let our own practice of those keep us from God's promises. Often, we feel our worst when we're the closest to God's blessings. So, Moses' story is a cautionary tale for us to stay focused, stay in the race, and finish well!

Lord, I need Your presence with me as I get closer to my finish line. Don't let me stumble mere yards from finishing. Uphold me when I am tired, weak, and despondent. Help me to look ahead and see Your promised blessings. In Jesus' name. Amen.

---

[1] *That Will Never Work: The Birth of Netflix and the Amazing Life of an Idea*, by Marc Randolph (Back Bay Books, 2022); page 252.

13

Lesson 13
Finishing Well
Deuteronomy 34

Preparing for the End

He didn't win the race, but in defeat, John Stephen Akhwari represented something much more profound and enduring than many star athletes achieve.

Before the 1968 Olympics in Mexico City, Akhwari, a native of Tanzania, was just another marathon runner. He had won marathons in Africa, running with times under two and a half hours, so he easily qualified for the Olympics. But in Mexico City, Akhwari encountered an obstacle he had never faced before. The altitude there caused his legs to cramp severely. Still, he kept running.

About halfway through the 26-mile marathon, Akhwari was involved in a melee of athletes jockeying for position. He tangled with other runners and fell. He dislocated his knee, scraped up his leg, and smashed his shoulder against the pavement. Most observers, seeing his injuries, assumed he would pull out of the race and go to the hospital. Instead, he received medical attention and returned to the race. With terrible injuries and cramped muscles slowing him, Akhwari labored on. His pace was now much slower, but his resolve to complete the event remained intact.

By the time Akhwari approached the finish line, nearly two hours later, the official timekeepers had put away their watches, and the awards ceremony was already under way. When the organizers were told there was still one runner laboring toward the finish line, the news was broadcast on local radio, and fans returned to the stands to cheer him on. The stadium lights were turned back on, and Akhwari ran the last lap to resounding applause.

With his leg bleeding and bandaged and a dislocated kneecap, Akhwari hobbled around the track, crossed the finish line, and collapsed. When a reporter asked him why he did not quit the race, he said, "My country did not send me 5,000 miles to start the race. They sent me 5,000 miles to finish it." Akhwari's perseverance and determination to finish the 1968 Olympic race has gone down in history as the greatest last-place finish in Olympic history.[1]

Moses, the great emancipator of Israel, was about to finish his race on earth. Like the people of Tanzania did not send John Stephen Akhwari 5,000 miles to start but not finish the race, God did not send Moses to start his race and not finish it. Though he stumbled near the end of his life, God picked him up so he could finish the race he started, and now he was poised to cross the finish line.

Moses' imminent death is a repeated theme in the closing chapters of the Book of Deuteronomy. The last months of Moses' life were filled with a lot of work. Besides leading Israel into the possession of Gilead,

According to the final chapter of Deuteronomy, Mount Nebo is where the Hebrew prophet Moses was given a view of the promised land that God was giving to the Jews. "And Moses went up from the plains of Moab to Mount Nebo, the top of Pisgah, which is opposite Jericho." (Deuteronomy 34:1). According to Jewish and Christian tradition, Moses was buried on this mountain by God himself, and his final resting place is unknown. Scholars continue to dispute whether the mountain currently known as Nebo is the same as the mountain referred to in the Torah. © Vyacheslav Argenberg

Moses had many other assignments, including reviewing the Law for the new generation of Israelites, copying down the Law in writing and giving it to the Levites for safekeeping, and then pronouncing the tribal blessings upon Israel. Once these tasks were completed, it was time for Moses' life to end.

Family members or friends write obituaries to summarize the life and character of a deceased loved one. Deuteronomy 34 is a short obituary of the greatest leader in the history of ancient Israel. Moses was preparing for death because he knew it was coming. He viewed death as an appointment that everyone must keep, so there is no way to avoid it. The best thing to do in the face of death is to be prepared for it.

Moses had begun his ministry as a lonely shepherd, caring for sheep near Horeb, the mountain of God. He would soon end his ministry, leaving his sheep, God's people, with Joshua as he went up Mount Nebo alone to meet God. Moses' siblings—Miriam and Aaron, along with the first generation of Hebrews—had already died, so there weren't many family members left to eulogize Moses. Only Joshua and Caleb remained.

1. How might John Stephen Akhwari's courageous story from the 1968 Olympic Games inspire you?

2. Moses' life was lived in three distinct phases of 40 years each. What phases of your life do you believe have been consequential? How did God use you in those phases?

3. Since death is an appointment none of us can avoid, how would you like to prepare yourself to meet God after this life?

A Preview of the Promise

"Then Moses went up from the plains of Moab to Mount Nebo, to the top of Pisgah, which is opposite Jericho, and the Lord showed him the whole land: Gilead as far as Dan, all Naphtali, the land of Ephraim and Manasseh, all the land of Judah as far as the Western Sea, the Negeb, and the Plain—that is, the valley of Jericho, the city of palm trees—as far as Zoar. The Lord said to him, 'This is the land of which I swore to Abraham, to Isaac, and to Jacob, saying, "I will give it to your descendants"; I have let you see it with your eyes, but you shall not cross over there' " (Deuteronomy 34:1-4).

As we read this passage, we can sense a measure of sadness. Moses had brought the people to the threshold of the Promised Land, but he had been denied admission because of his actions (Numbers 20). God said no to him and wouldn't allow him to enter the Promised Land, but there were many times across the span of Moses' life when God had said yes. God said yes to his need for help in confronting Pharaoh. God had said yes to Moses' request to see some part of God. God said yes to helping Moses lead the children of Israel out of Egypt and through the wilderness. But as Moses prepared to live through the last days of his life, God's answer was no.

God always answers our prayers and requests, but God may not give us the answer we want. There will be times when God says yes, but God is not obligated to grant our every wish and desire. God's plans transcend ours, so when we request something of God, our requests, though done in faith, do not supersede God's sovereign rule. There will be times in our lives when God will say no to us.

Instead of permitting Moses to enter the Promised Land with the new generation of Israelites, God took him to Mount Nebo, to the top of Pisgah, where God gave him a view of the land of Canaan. Moses had a view like no other. He saw all the way to the north as far as Dan, west as far as the Mediterranean Sea, southwest to the Negev, and down to Zoar on the southern tip of the Dead Sea. What Moses saw was not physically possible. Thus, he saw more than geography; he saw destiny.

In Deuteronomy 8, Moses described the land to the people as a land with abundant water, wheat, barley, fig trees, pomegranates, olive trees, and honey. In Chapter 34, God allows Moses to climb Mount Pisgah to see the land he had described to the people. There are two interesting features in verse 1.

Moses climbed up Mount Nebo to the top of Pisgah, and he saw a vast amount of land promised by God to his ancestors. In the first part of verse 7, we are told that Moses was 120 years old when he died. This was not exceptionally old at that time. Moses' father, Aram, lived to be 137; his grandfather Kohath lived to be 133; his great-grandfather Levi lived to be 137; and his great-great-grandfather Jacob lived to be 147.

Moses' 120 years were divided into three distinct 40-year periods. His first 40 years were spent in Egypt in Pharaoh's house as he was being raised as an adopted son of Pharaoh's daughter. The second 40 years of his life were lived in Midian as a shepherd. The third and final 40 years were spent leading Israel out of Egypt, through the wilderness, near the Promised Land.

Thus, the first 80 years of Moses' life were times of preparation. The first 40 years were preparation in the palace. The second 40 years were preparation in the pasture. Then, after 80 years of preparation, Moses was finally ready to lead Israel out of Egypt. We often complain about how long it may take for God to prepare us for our assignment; but the greater the work, the greater the preparation.

But we are in good company. In studying the Bible, we see that God took years to prepare the people God called to achieve God's will. We might feel we are ready and prepared to serve, but there may be something about us or in us that we can't see. Only God can see it, and it may be a hinderance to God's plan.

Furthermore, God does not lay hands on anyone immediately. Rather, God takes time to equip and prepare us for the work He has ahead of us. God will never ask us to do something that God has not prepared us to do. The equipping process and the preparation may seem harsh at times, but the events that mold our lives have the possibility of preparing us for a greater task.

As an interesting side note, Moses at 120 years old climbed to the top of Pisgah to see the Promised Land. The summit of Mount Pisgah reaches a height of

The Promised Land

Canaan is an ancient name for an area centered on Palestine that was given to the children of Israel as the Promised Land. Scholars debate the origin of the term *Canaan*, but it may come from an old Semitic word meaning, "reddish purple," a reference to the purple or crimson dye produced in the area. Canaanites are believed to be descendants of Ham, one of the sons of Noah.[3] Described in Scripture as "a land flowing with milk and honey," the soil was rich for agriculture and shepherding, the mountains provided security and protection from the elements and their enemies, and the arid climate provided perfect conditions for livestock to thrive (Exodus 3:17; Numbers 13:27; Deuteronomy 8:6-9).[4]

4,500 feet, which is almost a mile. Although in biblical days, 120 was not that old, but there probably weren't many 120-year-old men climbing up a mountain almost a mile high who lived to tell the story. Moses did it, scrambling hand over hand. In addition to his strength to get to the top of the mountain, his sight was unimpaired because he had a vast view of the Promised Land (verse 7).

God preserved Moses' health, strength, and eyesight so that in the end, when Moses was ready to cross the finish line, he could climb 4,500 feet and then see with clear eyesight what God had promised. Although he would not enter the land, God made sure he saw it. God preserved his life until he saw the promise made to his ancestors. God will preserve our lives until God's promises are fulfilled. "The one who began a good work among you will bring it to completion by the day of Jesus Christ" (Philippians 1:6).

In the spring of 1968, The Reverend Dr. Martin Luther King Jr.

was organizing what was known as the Poor People's Campaign. But during the campaign, he took time off to travel to Memphis, Tennessee, to lead a demonstration in support of higher wages for the city's sanitation workers. At a rally on April 3, the day before he was assassinated, King said that God allowed him to go up the mountain and see the promised land.

Like Moses, King did not get to enter with the people he was leading. He died outside the promised land of racial justice. He may have had a premonition that his life would be cut short, but he also understood that movements of transformation take time and aren't limited to one person's life or ministry. He did his part, like Moses, and would enter a different Promised Land, one where we will never grow old or die.

When Moses stood on Mount Pisgah looking at the Promised Land, he saw how his efforts would bear fruit. In that moment, he realized his labor was not in vain. He had led a full and powerful life, and he had witnessed the salvation of God's people. He was saved by an Egyptian princess out of the Nile River. He lived as a runaway in the desert of Midian. God used him as an emancipator as he stood up for God against the most powerful pharaoh of his day. He performed miracles in Egypt. He heard Pharaoh give the order to let God's people go. He was able to watch as the people worshiped God through the first Passover meal in preparation for the journey across the desert to the Promised Land.

Moses witnessed when God separated the Red Sea so the people could cross over into safety. On the freedom side of the Red Sea, Moses had the rare and often painful privilege of beholding God as God worked with the people to grow them into the holy nation God knew they could become. Moses received the Ten Commandments. He rebuked, challenged, loved, and encouraged the people. He stood as a liaison between the people and God. He glimpsed God's glory. He delivered the bad news that the wandering generation who came out of Egypt would not enter the land of promise because of their rebellion, and he accepted the fact that he would not be allowed to enter it either.

1. How do you feel when God says no to your prayers and requests?

2. Moses was so close to the Promised Land but was not allowed to enter. Have you ever come close to a goal but not achieved it?
   What happened?

3. As you examine your life, what are the highs and lows you've experienced? Where in those instances do you see God's presence?

Crossing the Finish Line

Now, Moses stood on top of the mountain prepared to take his last breath. He had taken his final view of the Promised Land, and "then Moses, the servant of the LORD, died there in the land of Moab, at the LORD's command" (verse 5).

The Midrash, the rabbinic biblical interpretation, grants Moses a beautiful death. According to the Midrash, at the end, God leaned down from the heavens and ended Moses' life with a soft, gentle kiss: "So Moses, the servant of the Eternal, died there, in the land of Moab, at the command of the Eternal." The Hebrew reads, "*al pi Adonai*," translated as "by the mouth of the Eternal," hence, the legend about God kissing Moses at his moment of death. The Baptist preacher of London, Charles H. Spurgeon, said, "As a mother takes her child and kisses it, and then lays it down to sleep in its own bed; so, did the Lord kiss the soul of Moses away to be with him forever."[2]

According to the Midrash, God wept after Moses died, as did the heavens and the earth. "[Moses] was buried in a valley in the land of Moab, opposite Bethpeor, but no one knows his burial place to this day" (verse 6). No one knows where Moses is buried because God buried Moses. There was no funeral, eulogy, flowers, or resolutions. However, he had the honor of having God perform his burial. When the time came for him to bring his journey to an end, God did not vanish from the scene. God accompanied him to the mountain and stayed with him until he took his last breath.

God's care for Moses on the mountain makes an important statement to us. The psalmist affirmed that the Lord considers the death of his children to be precious. In Psalm 116:15, the psalmist states, "Precious in the sight of the Lord is the death of his saints." Our lives are precious to God. While we're living, we serve God, but what value can a dying person have for God? We can no longer serve God, and we can no longer do what God commands once we breathe our last breath. From our perspective, death doesn't have the same value.

But the Lord has a different perspective on the death of the children of God. We matter to God when life surges within us, and God cares about us just as much when life leaves us. While we live, we enjoy God's presence. When we die, we can count on the blessing of God's company then as well. God considers us just as precious in dying as God does when we are living. Whether living or dying, we are precious in God's sight.

Moses will always be remembered as the only man buried by God. God buried him and laid him to rest in an unmarked tomb. When God buried Moses, God did not place a prominent tombstone at the grave to mark the site. Rather, God kept the site so secret that no one has ever discovered where Moses was buried. In the Book of Jude, we find an interesting statement concerning Moses' body. Following Moses' death, the archangel Michael and Satan contended over Moses' body (verse 9). It is uncertain exactly what they were arguing about or why Satan wanted the body.

While somewhat unclear, the dispute highlights the importance of Moses and all that he did for God's people. The Bible never states that Satan wanted anyone else's body. In the end, God denied Satan's request and buried Moses Himself in an undisclosed location.

Those who study the Bible speculate that perhaps Satan knew the idolatrous tendencies of the Israelites, and he wanted to put Moses' body in a location where the people would be tempted to build a shrine and eventually worship him. God knew that if God had not concealed Moses' grave, the valley of Beth-peor would have become a place of pilgrimage. Thus, it is believed that Michael was sent to intercept Satan before he could accomplish his wicked purpose.

However, there is absolutely nothing to be gained by speculating on what happened to Moses' body. He died, God buried him, and that's all we need to know. Nothing else is important. What can be more important than to know that when we come to the end of our journey God will be with us?

Verse 8 says, "The Israelites wept for Moses in the plains of Moab thirty days; then the period of mourning for Moses was ended." It was probably not until Moses died that some of the people realized how important he was to Israel and how much he, through the power of God, had done for them. How often it is that we never appreciate our blessings until we lose them?

Rabbi Sidney Greenberg wrote about what happened after the *Mona Lisa* was stolen from the Louvre Museum in Paris in 1911. The museum was closed for nine days, the French border was closed, and all departing ships and trains were searched. Greenberg noted that the painting was missing for two years. When the museum finally reopened, thousands of people lined up to see the empty spot on the wall where the painting once hung. More people went to the museum to stare at the blank space where the *Mona Lisa* once hung than had looked at the masterpiece in the five years before it was stolen.

Greenberg said that we tend not to recognize precious things while we have them. Only when they are taken away do we become painfully aware of the blank space in our lives, and our attention is sharply focused on that blank space. "The walls of our lives are crowded with *Mona Lisas*, but we are unmindful of them,"[5] that is until they are removed from our lives. It is important that we appreciate the people in our lives while we have them because at any moment they can be taken away.

After we discover who will carry the baton after Moses' death (verse 9), we read Moses' short but beautiful obituary: "Never since has there arisen a prophet in Israel like Moses, whom the LORD knew face to face. He was unequaled for all the signs and wonders that the LORD sent him to perform in the land of Egypt, against Pharaoh and all his servants and his entire land, and for all the mighty deeds and all the terrifying displays of power that Moses performed in the sight of all Israel" (verses 10-12).

The Book of Deuteronomy and Moses' life close with this incredible epitaph. God writes on Moses' tombstone, "Never since has there arisen a prophet in Israel like Moses." This was not because Moses performed mighty wonders. Many prophets would come after Moses, and there would be many signs and mighty acts of terror against the enemies of God. Even Joshua would experience signs and wonders, as would Elijah and Elisha. But no other human prophet would know God face to face.

What will people say about our lives when we die? More important, what will God say about our lives? Moses was sent by God, not just to start a race, but to finish it; and Moses did just that. Today, God is looking for faithful finishers. It doesn't matter if we've fallen or if we stumble at the finish line. God wants us to finish. Somewhere in life is a finish line we all must press toward and cross. Most of us want to believe that our finish line is years down the road. But no matter when we meet that finish line, we should strive to finish and finish well.

1. What do you want God to say about your life?

2. How can you be sure you will finish well?

3. In what ways has Moses' life inspired you?

Reflect and Pray

As our study of Moses' life comes to an end, we have a lot to reflect on for our own lives. As we review Moses's life, we can see how God guided, protected, and cared for him. From his birth under a pharaoh's cruel reign to his ascent of Mount Nebo to glimpse the Promised Land, we've explored the phases of Moses life and how God used violence, slavery, fear, and disobedience to bring about God's divine will for the deliverance of the children of Israel.

At the end of his life, Moses was prepared to meet his God. Although he, along with the original Exodus generation, did not cross over into the Promised Land, he did cross his own finish line. And it's certain that God received Moses and said, "Well done!"

Lord, I don't know where my life's finish line is, but when I cross it, I want to finish well. I want to live a life pleasing to You, a life that will witness to Your love, power, and salvation. Guide me on my life's journey so that when I reach the end of my life, I will be received into Your hands. In Jesus' name. Amen.

---

[1] "Marathon Man Akhwari Demonstrates Superhuman Spirit," Olympics.com (March 30, 2021).
[2] "The Death of Moses," sermon by Charles Haddon Spurgeon (June 5, 1887), *Metropolitan Tabernacle Pulpit*, Volume 33.
[3] "Canaan," *Encyclopedia Britannica*.
[4] "The Promised Land," by Annette Griffin, Bible Study Tools (November 30, 2021).
[5] *Say Yes to Life: A Book of Thoughts for Better Living*, by Sidney Greenberg (Jason Aronson, Inc., 1999); page 136.

www.ingramcontent.com/pod-product-compliance
Lightning Source LLC
Chambersburg PA
CBHW020420010526
44118CB00010B/335